Cooking with Vegetables

Cooking with Vegetables

Jesse Jenkins

A.D.I.P. (Another Day in Paradise)

BLUEBIRD

Contents

introduction

This isn't a vegetarian or vegan cookbook – I love to eat meat and fish and am a fan of a perfect steak. But it *is* a book about cooking vegetables in fresh and exciting ways to make them the hero of a meal. While many of the recipes you'll find in here use ingredients like anchovies, smoked bacon or chorizo, they're added not as the main event (and can be left out) but as accents to season, enhance flavour and add depth.

So why a vegetable-focused cookbook from a carnivore? For two reasons. First, I want to eat more vegetables myself so I'm always looking for ways to make them more irresistible. Second, my vegetable recipes just seem to resonate the most. They're the dishes that get huge views online and are shared and recreated by people around the world. People want to eat more plants both for themselves and for the planet, so I set aside my meat-eating ego and leaned into creating vegetable-led recipes with the same respect, craft and flavour usually saved for the main event.

Many of us grew up at a time when a main meal meant a cut of meat, a side of potatoes, and some steamed (or boiled) vegetables, particularly in the UK. This book is about breaking that mould and bringing vegetables to the forefront in ways that are anything but an afterthought. You'll find some of the dishes are light and fresh, with nourishment front of mind, and others are indulgent, decadent and downright filthy.

I approach cooking vegetables much like I would a piece of meat or fish. I start with one vegetable I'm excited to eat – ideally something in season – and build the meal around it. From there, I look for the most flavourful, interesting way to bring it to life. Sometimes that means charring it over an open flame for a smoky depth, other times it's steaming it until tender before searing to achieve a caramelised crust. In this book, you'll see how cooking vegetables in stages can bring out layers of flavour and texture, transforming humble ingredients like cabbage, leeks or carrots into something truly extraordinary.

I am a big condiment guy and so I often want to bring in a sauce – maybe a salsa verde or something spicy, sticky and sweet – then I think about what I want to serve the vegetable with: it could be a simple bowl of steaming rice or a bed of creamy beans. Then there's nearly always a sharply dressed salad or crunchy slaw to bring freshness. For me, adding 'freshness' to a dish is like rolling down the windows in a hot car and feeling the cool air stream in. It should balance the core flavour and complete the experience. Like the quarter lemon you squeeze over a white fish that's covered in capers and butter or the sweet and sour pickles on a burger, or the pile of herbs, chillies with fresh lime juice that cut through the bone broth in a bowl of pho.

I grew up in Los Angeles, California, and becoming a professional skateboarder was all I ever thought about. I pretty much lived on a board and worked in restaurants in the evenings to keep that dream alive. It was in the bustle of these LA kitchens that I fell in love with cooking. Many of the chefs I met over the years have a similar vibe to the people I skated with – intense perfectionists, soulful and often wildly entertaining. Cooking, like skateboarding, quickly became something I wanted to either be doing or watch others do. The most thrilling and challenging part of both skateboarding and cooking is that it's not just what you do, but how you do it. On a skateboard, so much is about personal style, and in cooking, two nearly identical plates can taste worlds apart. It all comes down to the details. These small, seemingly imperceptible differences can elevate a dish with a quality you can't quite put your finger on.

My palate was also broadened at this time – I had always consumed a lot of fast food on the road with skateboarding but a spell living next to Koreatown introduced me to ingredients like gochujang and kimchi, which you will see appear a lot in this book. The daily 'family meal' prepared by chefs for the restaurant teams I was part of also meant I got a deep appreciation for the flavours and processes of Hispanic food, and the love has stayed with me and influenced the way I eat forever.

Although I learned my techniques in professional kitchens, these recipes are very much for home cooking. No intimidating machines or overly complicated processes, just attention, time, and bold, focused flavours.

We all know that we should be cooking seasonally where possible – it is better for the planet and often tastier, fresher and more nutritious, as the ingredients haven't travelled so far to get to us. Local and seasonal food is also less likely to be coated in wax or contain preservatives, so check the label on your produce when you buy it to see where it was grown. If you can afford it (and are organised enough to get those beautiful boxes of vegetables delivered from local farms) that is excellent, but I'm keenly aware that most of us (me included) are usually cooking with produce and ingredients from the closest supermarket to home and so everything in this book should be easy enough to find and affordable. All this to say, get whatever version of the vegetable is most accessible to you – if it is heirloom or organic, good for you. For these recipes it doesn't matter at all if it isn't.

I have organised this book by types of easy-to-find vegetables rather than by where they go on the table, side, main or snack, or what time of day to eat them. I want the focus to stay on what you feel like eating and then enjoy making it into something delicious. Where the dish ends up on your table, or when you choose to eat it, is entirely up to you. After all, a vegetable is only a side dish if you put it there.

Despite being a big dessert eater, I'm not really a big dessert maker. I've prepared many whilst working in restaurants, but not so many at home. The super precise measuring, countertop mess and time it takes always put me off. The dessert that I usually like to serve friends is paletas (Mexican popsicles) and I've included my favourite recipe for those in the final chapter. The others you'll find here are more of a compilation of my most loved cakes, puddings and desserts that have been made for me by my closest people. Some of them are family recipes that have been shared around and tweaked over the years. That is my ideal kind of sweet treat – not 'show-offy' or fine dining but simple, easy-to-get-right and made to share around a table of people you love.

When I cook for myself, I tend to recreate some kind of 'fast food', whether it's a quick noodle bowl, a curry and rice or a crispy fried sandwich. These dishes are typically designed for one or two people, making them easy to prepare on a hectic day. But when I'm cooking for a bigger group, my goal is to make the meal interactive and fun – I love food that invites people to reach across the table, share and experiment with different combinations. You'll find plenty of dishes you can mix and match when eating communally. After all, the best meals aren't only about what's on the plate – they're about how we share them with others.

I hope you enjoy,

JJ x

tools

I am a minimalist by nature, so try to only have what I need in life and this is especially true with cooking. I like to have tools that are similar to the ones used in professional kitchens because they are usually reasonably priced, hard-wearing and have simple utilitarian designs. Having the right kit can make cooking easier and having too much does the opposite. Finding the balance of having the least amount of kit while also having everything you need is the goal. Sometimes that means having to buy an expensive pan (that will last a lifetime) or it can mean using a £20 catering bread knife for all of your cutting, because it always works and doesn't need sharpening.

Taking the time to look at your process, thinking about where would be easiest to reach for utensils and what you need in that space, can completely change the experience of cooking. Cleaning as you go is life-changing in my experience. I was a very untidy kid (and adult). Learning how to get ahead of that and never feeling like a giant mess is looming ahead of me, only little ones as I go, has helped me grow as a cook. No matter what I say, it's about your experience in the kitchen, so use the tools that work for you and keep you cooking. Here are a few that I depend on:

Utensils

I use stainless steel or wood utensils. They impart very little flavour to the food if any, and last a lifetime if looked after properly. Plastic and silicone have their uses, but I try to avoid them because of the way they absorb flavours and constantly need replacing. I worked for a chef who made us taste all the plastic/silicone spatulas in a kitchen to make a point, and it totally worked on me. Some tasted like soap, some like onions, some of a little bit of everything.

Mandoline

I often use a mandoline. I know it can be a scary tool, but once you get used to it, the chance of injury becomes similar to the risks you take when using a knife. Consider using a guard or glove. They make light work of preparing vegetables and achieve a wafer-thin slice that's hard to match. It's my go-to tool for making slaws or raw vegetable salads because it's fast and the texture is unbeatable, in my opinion.

Knives

A chef's knife and a bread knife will cover most home cooks' needs. Try to keep your knives sharp – it's safer to have a sharp knife than a dull one. Dull knives require you to use more pressure when cutting, and if you make a mistake while applying pressure you could have a big problem. A steel chef's knife and a basic two-stage pull-through sharpener will do the trick.

Kitchen Scissors

If I can find a way to cut something with scissors and avoid cleaning my cutting board, I do. Roughly chopped herbs, spring onions, or for anything oily like a kimchi pancake, I use a solid set of kitchen scissors and sharpen them with the same sharpener as I use for my knife.

Speed Peeler

I have a speed peeler, or a Y peeler with replaceable blades. Other than the obvious stuff, like peeling off vegetable skins, I'll use it to ribbon vegetables for a salad, or shave cheese. It bums me out when I see someone roughly dragging a dull peeler over a carrot: be nice to your vegetables and try to replace the blades of your peeler when they become dull, the same as you would the razor in your bathroom.

Microplane Grater

A microplane is another tool that makes light work of boring tasks like chopping garlic or ginger, as well as being the best tool for zesting citrus fruit and grating hard cheeses. It's an essential for me.

Pots and Pans

I could write an essay on pots and pans but no one has asked me to, yet. More than anything, I just avoid using non-stick pans unless it's totally necessary. Besides essentially cooking on plastic, their coatings wear off and they become terrible pans. I keep one non-stick pan on hand for when I find myself having serious trouble with something sticking, like a kimchi pancake or a Spanish tortilla. Everything else happens in steel or cast iron. It takes some learning, but it all becomes second nature very quickly. Cast iron has the best 'non-stick' quality, so I cook things like eggs or pancakes with it. Most jobs are interchangeable as far as steel or cast iron go, though it's best to avoid cooking acidic foods like wine or tomatoes in cast iron, as they can strip away the seasoning (but a little is okay). It's not the end of the world if that happens as you can re-season it. That's the beauty of real pans, they can take a beating and be brought back to life. I love the idea of my kids being able to use our pans when I'm gone and keep that in mind whenever I'm tempted by another 'non-stick' gimmick. Lastly, I'll often transfer my pan from the stove to the oven to finish cooking, and that's never an issue with steel and cast iron (as long as they don't have wooden handles).

I mostly use a standard set of steel saucepans, a steel sauté pan with a lid, a steel frying pan, a cast-iron skillet and a large casserole dish with a lid. You don't need all of these to cook my recipes but it's a good reference for what's necessary and useful in a cook's kitchen.

pantry

This is not a list of things that are hard to find, this section is simply here to highlight the pantry ingredients that are key players in my recipes and would be great to have in your cupboard. Condiments as well as foods that are fermented, pickled or brined, can take your cooking to the next dimension, and if they are not already familiar to you, I hope to make them an extension of your cooking hand.

Miso
I mostly use a sweet white miso/shiro miso. It's sweet because it's fermented for less time, and has a subtler flavour than the darker varieties. It's one of my favourite ingredients for adding deep savouriness to cooking. Its emulsification properties make it perfect for bringing sauces together or thickening a stew. Once you understand its abilities it becomes a total weapon.

Dijon Mustard
Dijon mustard has many uses in cooking beyond spreading on a sandwich. Having a good one to hand is non-negotiable. When I say good one, I just mean one that you love the taste of, and for me, that's any classic French brand.

Soy Sauce and Fish Sauce
Soy sauce is often listed as an ingredient without specifying what type, and there are big differences in flavour and quality. I mostly use a Chinese light soy sauce, or a Japanese soy sauce in my cooking.

Chinese for Chinese-inspired dishes, and Japanese for Japanese – this might sound obvious, but I do see people interchange them. Try to buy a premium brand that says 'naturally brewed' – the second ingredient should be soybeans, with no artificial ingredients.

If you've been put off using fish sauce in the past, it's worth trying. I prefer to use fish sauce that only has two or three ingredients – fish, salt and sugar. The brand Red Boat is my favourite.

Oil
I use olive oil, extra virgin olive oil, rapeseed oil and toasted sesame oil in my cooking. I don't care what anyone says to you, you absolutely can use olive oil for cooking. I cook with it unless I don't want something to taste like it, or if I'm deep frying. You can deep fry with olive oil, it's just expensive and usually doesn't make sense for me flavour-wise. I use a reasonably priced olive oil for cooking and a grassy, peppery extra virgin olive oil for dressings, and finishing dishes. When I list neutral oil in a recipe, I'm talking about oils with little to no flavour, that have high smoke points. Rapeseed/canola oil is my go-to, but make sure it's refined, as the unrefined versions don't have the same smoke point and are for finishing dishes (similar to an extra virgin olive oil). Toasted sesame oils can vary in taste, so I like to use a high-quality Chinese brand – they can be expensive but a little goes a long way.

Vinegar

You can go very deep when it comes to vinegar, and if you're an acid lover it's an ingredient worth exploring. One of my favourite vinegars is Moscatel and is worth trying. I mostly use white wine, apple cider or rice vinegar for my cooking and choose them 100% for their taste, not price or origin. I also have a nice red wine vinegar, a Chinese black vinegar/Chinkiang, and a good aged balsamic in my pantry. It's a bit of an arsenal, but the white vinegars are pretty interchangeable – if I had to pick one it would probably be either white wine or rice.

Capers, Olives and Cornichons

I don't feel okay unless I know that these three ingredients are in my kitchen. They can transform simple meals and give them a quiet backbone, especially when you use their brines as well. Try to get high quality across all three (the cornichons just do need to be French, in my opinion).

Anchovies, Smoked Bacon/Lardons and Chorizo

A small amount of any of these adds a lot of flavour, and I'll often use them in vegetable-focused meals. Vegetables tend to be sweet, and these ingredients can add savouriness without overpowering everything. They are not essential, but if you're not vegetarian, they can help keep more vegetables at the centre of your meals.

White Wine and Stock

A big difference between restaurant cooking and home cooking is often wine and stock. Most restaurant sauces have a stock in them, which I know takes time, but they are easy to make at home. We have a roast chicken most weeks in our house, so any leftovers and vegetable trimmings go in a big pot with some herbs and peppercorns, and then it bubbles away for the day. I freeze it, usually in ice cube trays, or deli containers. You just add it straight from frozen at the same time as you would normally add stock, or it keeps in the fridge for 3–4 days. Wine plays a similar role, and I'll often use it in combination with stock. Try to use an affordable wine you like the taste of, and avoid anything sweet. I use a dry white wine and will also freeze it in ice cube trays rather than have the bottle sitting in my fridge once it's opened.

Salt and Sugar

I regularly use a balance of salt and sugar to season dishes that are acidic. It should help all the best qualities come out. If I'm seasoning a dish with vinegar, I'll usually add a pinch of (any) sugar but leave that out if it's not working for you.

pickles
and
ferments

This is one of the easiest recipes you will ever make. Other than time, there is nothing to it. When you see how short the ingredients list is, you might be tempted to add other flavours, but I urge you not to! If you fully commit to the flavour of the chilli, you can be rewarded with an inarguably perfect hot sauce. Some of the world's most popular vinegar-based hot sauces only have 2-3 ingredients listed - it's the type of chilli and the process of fermentation that gives them their unique taste. I like to use red Fresno chillies, but if you want it spicier you can add a habanero or some bird's-eye. Use this recipe to make as much or as little sauce as you'd like.

fermented chilli sauce

red chillies (Fresno), trimmed,
   sliced in half lengthways
garlic, peeled and crushed
   whole
3% salt
vinegar

I normally add one clove of garlic for every 10 chillies.

Place your jar on a scale and zero it out. Add the chillies, garlic and enough water to cover, then add 3% of the total weight in salt. Mix well, then cover with a fermentation weight and seal. Leave to ferment for 1-3 weeks.

Strain the chillies, reserving a few spoons of the brine. Put them into a blender with 1-2 spoons of brine, then blitz until smooth. Season with 1-2 spoons of rice vinegar, and a pinch of sugar (optional).

Water, salt, time, and an oxygen-free environment. I try and keep that simple definition of fermentation in my head, as it can be intimidating. I don't have endless shelves of bubbling jars in my house, I'm not an all-in fermenter, but there are a few that I love to make. Kimchi, sauerkraut, and chilli sauce are my usuals, and between these three recipes, you can get a good handle on the process. If you want to make your life easier, get a few jars with fermentation lids, and a couple of fermentation weights. You can absolutely make do without them, but you will have less drama if you have them. After coming home to an exploded sauerkraut or two I got the gear.

My mom lived very close to K-town (Korea town) in LA, so grew up eating a lot of incredible Korean food. My mom loved Korean BBQ in particular, and we would all go on special occasions. At first, I would mostly eat grilled meat but over time I started to be more interested in the banchan (side dishes that are often pickles and ferments). I also got to eat a lot of home-cooked Korean food at friends' houses, so my love for it runs deep.

I learned how to make 'Mak Kimchi' – rough/careless kimchi – it's faster and easier than most napa cabbage kimchi recipes and perfect for the home cook.

careless kimchi

FILLS TWO 1-LITRE JARS OR CONTAINERS

1.5kg napa cabbage
1 large carrot
1 small daikon (or any radish)
1 bunch spring onion

BRINE

50g sea salt
750ml water

PASTE

½ white onion
1 green apple
4-6 garlic cloves
25g ginger, skinned
2 tbsp fish sauce
30–70g gochugaru
  (depending on how spicy
  you like it)
25-50g fermented shrimp
1 tsp sugar

Dissolve the sea salt in water.

Remove the core from the cabbage and cut it into roughly 6cm chunks - put them into a large bowl. Pour over the brine in layers, mix well and leave to sit for 2 hours - mixing it every 30 minutes.

Put the onion, apple, garlic, and ginger into a food processor and blitz until smooth. Transfer it to a large bowl with the fish sauce, gochugaru, chopped fermented shrimp, and sugar, then mix well.

Slice the carrot, and radish into thin slices, about the size of matchsticks. Cut the spring onions into 2.5cm pieces. Add to the bowl of paste.

Rinse the cabbage three times with cold water, then add to the bowl and give it a good mix, making sure everything is covered with the paste. You can eat it fresh like this, it's a bit salty and punchy but I love it.

Put it into an airtight container and leave it at room temp for 1-2 days, then keep it in the fridge and enjoy. It will become sourer one week to the next, and when it's very sour it's best for things like kimchi stew, Korean pancake, or fried rice.

I mostly use the classic 3-2-1 method for making pickle brine. It's a quick and easy way of pickling vegetables and fruit that you have to hand. The order is interchangeable, but I usually use three parts vinegar, two parts water and one part sugar – by weight. This makes sweet and sour pickles that are super versatile, and it's just a moreish way to eat more vegetables. Putting half a fennel bulb in your sandwich might sound weird, but if it is sweet, sour and crunchy then it is killer.

Round up or down to make measurements easier. You don't have to be precious about the proportions (experiment with your brines – you can always reduce the sugar to your tastes). I sometimes make excess pickling liquid and bottle it to finish dishes or add to dressings. If you want to avoid any excess, the easiest way to measure it is to fill your container with what you plan to pickle, place it on a scale and fill it with water. Use the overall weight to get your measurements, then just make sure your 3-2-1 components don't weigh more in total than the weight of the water.

Use whatever vinegar you like the taste of most – I mostly use rice vinegar, cider vinegar or white wine vinegar. If you are pickling something sweet, I would also add a big pinch of salt.

These two recipes give you an overview of the process, and there are plenty more here – see Bread and Butter Pickles on page 33 and Pickled Carrot on page 231. They all keep in the fridge for a very long time: crunchy vegetables tend to last for what feels like forever, but softer ones do start to break down over time regardless. If stored properly in airtight containers they don't go off for upwards of a year, if not longer.

3-2-1 pickles

pickled fennel

fennel bulbs, stalks removed,
  bulbs quartered or cut into
  eighths
3 parts rice vinegar
2 parts caster sugar
1 part water
fennel seeds
black peppercorns
salt

Put pieces of fennel in a bowl, season generously with salt, mix, then leave at room temperature for 1 hour.

Drain the excess water and give them a good rinse with cold water, then put them in clean containers.

Bring the vinegar, sugar, water and spices to the boil in a saucepan, then cover the fennel with the hot liquid. Leave to cool at room temperature, seal and store in the fridge (a little goes a long way with the spices, just ¼ teaspoon fennel and a couple of black peppercorns for 3 fennel bulbs would be fine).

quick pickled chilli

salt
sugar
fresh chillies of choice, sliced
  or chopped
white or red vinegar of
  choice

Combine equal parts salt and sugar in a bowl. Stir in the chillies and leave for 5–10 minutes, then cover with any white or red vinegar. Leave for 10 minutes, then it's ready to use.

My last meal would be a sandwich with B&B pickles. I have a happy childhood memory of sitting on the beach wrapped in a towel, still wet and a little cold, eating a sandwich made of cheap white bread, mayonnaise, mustard, bologna and B&B pickles – adding crisps to each bite as I went. I was told that the name 'bread and butter' dates back to the American Depression, when these pickles were a cheap way to make a plain sandwich taste better. They're always in my fridge. They are great to have simply on the side of most savoury meals to brighten things up. My grandpa liked to have them with French fries, one of my favourite combinations.

bread and butter pickles

FILLS A 1-LITRE JAR

6 Persian cucumbers,
   or 3 English
1 white onion
2 red chillies
1 tsp white mustard seeds
1 tsp celery seeds
1 tsp black peppercorns
3–6 cloves (depending on
   your taste – go easy on
   them, as they are very
   intense)
1 tsp ground turmeric
600ml vinegar
300g light brown sugar
200ml water
sea salt

Slice the cucumbers, onion and chillies to your desired thickness and shape. There is no right way here, but it is worth thinking about how you intend to eat them. I like thick coins for the cucumbers and the same for the onion and chilli. If you want the flavour of chilli but not pieces throughout, cut them in half and add them to the mix.

Once cut, put the vegetables into a large bowl and season generously with salt – every piece should have a good amount on it. Mix, then cover and leave to sit in the fridge for at least 2 hours. I normally leave mine for about 4 hours. This process 'cures' and draws out moisture from the vegetables, giving you a crunchy pickle.

Drain the vegetables and rinse well with cold water to wash off excess salt. Leave in a colander in the sink to keep draining.

Put the whole spices into a dry saucepan large enough to accommodate the pickling liquid. Lightly toast the whole spices before adding the turmeric, vinegar, sugar and water. Mix well and let it come to the boil, make sure the sugar has dissolved, then add the cucumber, onion and chilli to the boiling liquid and turn off the heat. Cover the pan with a lid and leave to cool to room temperature. Transfer to clean jars, seal and keep in the fridge – they last for a good few months if kept cool, but you'll eat them long before they go off.

If you haven't been to a spot that serves 'Korean army stew', please make it happen. It's one of my all-time favourite meals to share with friends. A big pot of bubbling goodness with toppings to keep everyone happy. It reminds me of all the ways I used to 'pimp out' packet ramen when I was growing up. So much time and love go into making kimchi, and although this stew comes together quickly, it has a deeply delicious flavour.

kimchi and butter bean stew

SERVES **4–5**

1–2 tbsp gochujang
1–2 tbsp gochugaru
2–4 garlic cloves, minced
1 tbsp light soy sauce
1 tbsp caster sugar
800ml water, vegetable stock
  or dashi
300g kimchi, plus 2 tbsp juice
1 floury potato, peeled and
  thinly sliced
400g tin butter beans,
  drained
4 large spring onions, thinly
  sliced, or to taste

OPTIONAL ADD-INS AND
  TOPPINGS

fresh enoki mushrooms
medium-firm tofu, diced
Korean rice cakes
1 packet ramen noodles,
  cooked
American cheese slices
eggs

Make a paste with the gochujang, gochugaru, minced garlic, soy sauce and sugar – this is your soup base. It's helpful to make it a couple of hours before, to allow the ingredients to get to know each other and balance the flavour.

Put the water, vegetable stock or dashi in a saucepan, add the soup base, kimchi and juice and the sliced potato and bring to the boil. Cook for about 10 minutes, and when the potato slices are soft, add the beans and reduce the heat. Simmer for a couple of minutes, then add the spring onions, any extra add-ins and toppings, and you're good to go. I always have rice cakes, tofu and eggs – simply cracked in and poached in the broth – with this stew.

The first time I had this combination was in Stockholm, and it totally blew my mind. It's an obvious combo when you think about it – melted cheese and pickles/ferments have been friends for a long time – but this had that extra special kimchi spice and funk. Needless to say, it became a big part of my life and hopefully it will be part of yours too.

When I was a kid, we would dip our grilled cheese in tomato ketchup, so that desire runs deep in me. If you understand that feeling, I recommend you make the kimchi ketchup dip.

kimchi grilled cheese

SERVES 1

75g kimchi, finely chopped
50g mild cheddar, grated
50g grated mozzarella
1 tbsp gochujang
fresh cracked black pepper
1 tbsp softened butter
2 slices sourdough bread

FOR THE KIMCHI KETCHUP DIP

100g ketchup
100g kimchi with its juice
2 tbsp gochujang (optional)

Yes, I'm going to get bossy about grilled cheese. If it's being made with sourdough bread it needs to be cooked low and slow with some weight on top. This can be a chef's press or a heavy pan, as long as it's a fair amount smaller than the pan you're cooking in, so you don't create a lot of steam. Unless you are working with pre-sliced cheese, it should be made with grated cheese, and no, I don't mind if it's pre-grated, I love that stuff.

When it comes to the kimchi grilled cheese, it's important that the kimchi is chopped up a bit. When the cabbage heats up, it absorbs moisture and gets mouth-burning hot. Chopping it finely and mixing it with the grated cheese ensures everything cooks at the same time and you don't have to bite through any big chunks.

Mix the chopped kimchi, grated cheeses and gochujang in a bowl with some freshly cracked black pepper. Spread an even layer of butter on the surface of both slices of bread.
continued overleaf...

kimchi grilled cheese *(continued)*

Build the sandwich in a cold heavy-based pan (I use cast iron or carbon steel – other pans will work, just keep a close eye as they heat up more quickly and the sandwich can burn more easily): place a piece of bread buttered side down in the cold pan, spread the kimchi and cheese mixture over the bread (allowing 2cm space around the edge) then top with the second slice of bread, buttered side up. Making sure there is about 2cm of space around the edge helps stop it spilling over as soon as it melts.

Place a weight on top and cook over a medium-low heat for at least 5 minutes, I usually go for about 10 minutes, so it's as dark brown and crispy as possible. Flip and do the same on the other side.

Making the kimchi ketchup is a simple blending job: just make sure you blend the ingredients on high speed for at least a full minute – I do it for 2–3 minutes – to ensure a glossy sauce with a smooth texture.

You'll find sauerkraut in most organic health-food shops, but it is the easiest thing to make at home, and a lot cheaper too. My grandpa John grew cabbages in his garden, so sauerkraut was made every year. I loved hearing stories about him and my mom driving around the town in a car with no seatbelts, beers in hand (it was a different time), dropping jars off to their neighbours. One of my favourite sandwiches was my mom's version of a fried bologna sandwich. She would fry a few slices of mortadella until crispy and warm a big scoop of sauerkraut up in the rendered fat. Once warm she would put it on top of the mortadella, add American mustard and a few slices of provolone cheese. Once it was melted it would all go into a soft roll.

sauerkraut

FILLS ONE **500**ML JAR OR CONTAINER

500g halved and cored pale green or white cabbage
10g fine sea salt
2 garlic cloves, grated with a microplane grater
1 tsp juniper berries
½ tsp caraway seeds
½ tsp fennel seeds

Slice the cored cabbage as thinly or thickly as you like. I prefer to cut it into thin slices using a mandoline.

Weigh the sliced cabbage, then add 2% of its weight in salt (here, that's 10g salt for 500g cabbage). Mix it in well, then start to firmly massage it with clean hands, without breaking or crushing the slices. After a few minutes it will start to release some water and feel softer. Let it rest for 15 minutes at room temperature, then give it another massage, followed by another 15-minute rest.

Add the grated garlic and the spices, then mix well. Put the mix into a clean jar and cover with any liquid from the bottom of the bowl. Use a fermentation weight, or a sandwich bag filled with water, to create a water seal at the top. If you don't have a fermentation lid, 'burp' the jar (to release gas) once a day.

After about 2 weeks at room temperature, it's good to go. Keep it in the fridge after that – it will keep for months, for longer if well sealed.

This recipe went through so many iterations that by the end of it I almost didn't know what I was after. I was stuck between textures, as the intention was to make it as crispy as possible, but when you do that with one of these pancakes it loses something. You need the 'pancake' softness with crispy edges, but you don't want it to be soggy. This is my scrambled brain any time I am cooking with water and flour. I eventually found the right balance and feel like it's now foolproof enough for me to share the recipe with others. I pair this pancake with a Korean green onion salad – a typical Korean barbecue side dish – and a dipping sauce for extra deliciousness.

kimchi pancake

MAKES **1** LARGE PANCAKE FOR SHARING

2 tbsp neutral oil, for cooking the pancake
200g kimchi and 1 tbsp brine
2 spring onions, cut into 2.5cm pieces
½ white onion (60g), thinly sliced
40g plain flour
20g cornflour
40ml cold or iced water
salt

FOR THE GREEN ONION SALAD (PA MUCHIM)

6 spring onions, trimmed and cut into three pieces
3 tbsp light soy sauce
2 tsp caster sugar
1 tbsp gochugaru (Korean hot chilli flakes)
2 tbsp toasted white sesame seeds

FOR THE DIPPING SAUCE

2 tbsp light soy sauce
1 tbsp rice vinegar
1 tbsp water
1 tsp sugar

First, make the salad. Cut the spring onion pieces as thinly as possible lengthways, then soak them in cold water for 5 minutes. Drain well, then put the sliced spring onion in a bowl with the rest of the salad ingredients. Give it a good mix and set aside till the pancake is ready.

This is one of the rare occasions when I use a non-stick frying pan. The pancakes can be cooked in other pans but they require too much attention and are never as good as when I make them in a non-stick pan.

This comes together quickly, and you want your pan ready, oiled and hot when you go to mix the batter. Put your pan over a medium heat with the 2 tablespoons of oil.

Put the kimchi and its brine into a bowl, then use scissors to roughly chop it up. Add the spring onion, onion, flour, cornflour and a pinch of salt, then gently mix together. Add the cold water (I use iced water) and mix together until evenly combined, then pour the batter into the hot pan, pressing it into a pancake shape edge to edge. After about a minute, swirl the pan in a circular motion to make sure the oil is going across the whole surface. Cook for 5–7 minutes or until lightly golden, then flip and repeat on the other side. I drain mine on a wire rack but 30 seconds on a paper towel will do, just not longer as it will start to steam and get soggy.

I keep the dip pretty simple (just combine the ingredients in a bowl), as I've got the punchy salad doing its thing too.

Fried rice has been a staple of my diet since I was a teenager and it was one of the first things I learned to cook. This is not a traditional recipe, it's a version I made when trying to recreate a fancy restaurant one. I often have Pickled Ginger (see page 47) to hand but you can substitute that with fresh ginger, finely grated, and a pinch of sugar. I use leftover rice because the grains stay separated more easily, but you could also spread freshly cooked rice on a plate and leave it in the fridge uncovered for 20 minutes to chill before frying. Woks make frying easier but you can use a cast-iron or non-stick frying pan.

green chilli and pickled ginger fried rice

SERVES 2

4 green chillies
2 garlic cloves
4 tbsp neutral oil (I use rapeseed)
3 eggs, whisked
6 spring onions, thinly sliced and white and green parts kept separate
200g cooked long-grain rice
1 tsp light soy sauce
30g pickled ginger (shop-bought or see page 47), minced
MSG, to taste
white pepper
salt

Blend the green chillies and garlic in a small blender, food processor or with a pestle and mortar, and set aside.

Get the wok or frying pan smoking hot over a high heat, then add 2 tablespoons of the oil. Swirl it around the pan then pour the egg into the centre of the pan. Leave it for 20 seconds – it will quickly cook and form an almost unturned omelette – then break it apart with the back of a wooden spoon and transfer it to a plate.

Put the pan back over the heat and when it's smoking hot add another tablespoon of oil and swirl it around the pan. Add the white part of the spring onions and the chilli and garlic paste, stirring continuously for 30 seconds and making sure it doesn't burn. Add the rice, stirring continuously over a high heat for 1 minute, then add the egg and stir through. Spoon the soy sauce around the edge of the pan so it caramelises on the hot pan, then stir through. Remove from the heat once the rice is piping hot and add the pickled ginger, the green part of the spring onion, pinch of salt (or to taste), MSG and a pinch of white pepper, stir through and serve.

I often make this with tinned tuna and anchovies, but it's great without them. Kimchi is another funky, briny flavour that happily sits alongside the capers and olives. Almost all the intense flavour comes from vegetables (technically fruits, if you want to be annoying) that have been cooked or prepared in a way that homes in on their best qualities and makes them shine.

kimchi pasta puttanesca

SERVES **4**

4 tbsp extra virgin olive oil
500g cherry tomatoes
1 white onion, thinly sliced
4 garlic cloves, thinly sliced
6 tinned anchovy fillets in oil
1 tsp dried red chilli flakes
2 tbsp pitted olives (Italian
   black olives or whatever you
   prefer)
2 tbsp capers, drained
300g roughly-cut kimchi,
   plus 1 tbsp brine
1 tbsp white wine vinegar
pinch of caster sugar
100g tinned tuna in spring
   water, drained
300–400g spaghetti

TO SERVE (OPTIONAL)

handful of parsley, roughly
   chopped
lemon juice, to taste

Heat the oil in a large saucepan over a medium-high heat, then add the tomatoes and onion and cook for 7–10 minutes, or until you can pop the tomatoes with the back of your spoon. Add the garlic and anchovy and cook for a couple of minutes until fragrant, using the back of your spoon or a fork to break down the anchovy into the sauce. Add the chilli flakes, olives, capers, kimchi and brine, vinegar, sugar and tuna and cook for 2 minutes, then turn off the heat. You just want the last additions to be warmed through but not lose their bright, briny flavour.

Cook the spaghetti in a large pot of seasoned boiling water till al dente, then mix it through the sauce with a little of the pasta cooking water. You can add some parsley and fresh lemon juice before serving.

One of the best things about growing up in LA was the availability of incredible Mexican food and I miss it with all my heart. Everything from bubbling pots of barbacoa on street corners to Americanised chain drive-throughs – it all tastes good. LA also has 'strip malls' almost everywhere you look – small collections of stores, from food shops to cell-phone shops, massage parlours to nail salons, surrounding a small parking lot. In the area where I grew up there were often Mexican spots and Korean spots across the street from each other, and this dish was born when I added some kimchi and pickled chillies from the Korean spot to my Mexican rice and beans. It was and is the bomb. This one always gets two thumbs up from my old lady, and she said it had to go in the book.

black bean and kimchi salad

SERVES 3–4

100g brown rice or green
  lentils
2 sweetcorn cobs, if in season
  (otherwise use tinned, or
  leave out completely)
100g kimchi, plus 2 tbsp
  kimchi juice
20g pickled jalapeños, whole
  or roughly chopped
4 plum tomatoes, deseeded
  and diced
1 white onion, finely diced
4–6 spring onions, trimmed
  and thinly sliced, plus extra
  to serve
1 ripe avocado, stoned and
  sliced
handful of coriander, torn,
  plus extra to serve
juice of 2–3 limes
2–3 tbsp extra virgin olive oil
1 tsp caster sugar
1 head romaine or iceberg
  lettuce, leaves torn, roughly
  chopped or sliced
100g feta, crumbled
400g tin black beans,
  drained, rinsed and dried
salt

Cook the rice or lentils according to the packet instructions, then leave to cool to room temperature.

If the corn is in season, cut the kernels from the cob, rinse them and add them to the mix raw. If you prefer cooked corn, blanch the cobs in salted boiling water for 2–3 minutes, cool, then cut from the cob.

Put all the ingredients, other than the lettuce, rice, beans and feta, in a bowl with a good pinch of salt and a little pinch of sugar. Mix well and leave to sit at room temperature for 10–15 minutes.

Add the lettuce, cheese, rice (or lentils) and beans with some extra coriander and spring onion, mix and you're good to go. Check for seasoning, adding extra lime, salt or oil if needed. Some crushed tortilla chips added to this goes down very well too.

I love having pickled ginger in the house. As a teenager, a few of my friends got sponsored for skateboarding and started making some cash. We would all go out for sushi in LA as a group but I still couldn't afford it so I would order a bowl of rice and eat as much of the pickled ginger that accompanied their sushi as they would give me. It can be pretty expensive to buy, so I almost always make my own. Japanese recipes use young ginger, including the pink stems to create the colour you often see. Use young ginger if you can find it, but whatever you can buy will do.

pickled ginger

FILLS ONE 500ML JAR OR CONTAINER (WITH SOME SPARE PICKLING LIQUID TO SAVE FOR DRESSINGS)

150g fresh ginger (young, with pink stem intact, if possible)
300ml rice vinegar (or any white vinegar will work)
200ml water
100g caster sugar

Peel the ginger with the edge of a spoon (this removes less of the ginger and helps keep the shape of the root), trim the stem and cut the ginger into roughly 5cm-long pieces. Thinly slice into sheets or discs using a mandoline or sharp knife. Young ginger slices easier, and prettier – grown-up ginger gets a little more beat up as the fibres want to grab onto the blade – use the sharpest knife you have, or a fresh mandoline blade to ensure the slices are as clean and neat as possible.

Add the sliced ginger to a saucepan of boiling water, place over a medium heat and when it comes back to the boil strain the ginger. Spread it out over a plate or tray to cool. Sprinkle with salt and when it's cool enough to handle, squeeze as much moisture out as possible. Transfer to a clean, heatproof jar or other container.

Put the vinegar, water and sugar in a saucepan and bring to the boil, then pour the liquid over the ginger and leave to cool, loosely covered, at room temperature. Once cooled, it's good to go but I normally wait 24 hours. It will keep for up to a year in the fridge; just make sure you always use clean utensils to remove it from the jar.

My mother was an east coast American Italian, so I grew up with things like giardiniera – spicy pickled vegetables. They are a staple of any Italian-American diet and are often used in sandwiches. My version is a bit spicier than usual, and incorporates whatever vegetables I need to use up. You can pickle or ferment it – I normally pickle it as I have very little patience and I like it a little sweet.

giardiniera

FILLS A COUPLE OF JARS

150g cauliflower florets
  (1 medium/small head)
150g carrots, peeled
75g red pepper, deseeded
75g green beans, trimmed
75g celery stalks
75g pearl onions, peeled
50g red chillies (about 3)
4 garlic cloves, smashed or
  sliced
1 tsp fennel seeds
1 tsp black peppercorns
6 cloves
2 bay leaves
2 tsp dried chilli flakes
300ml distilled white vinegar
150ml water
25g caster sugar
salt

Cut all the vegetables into similar-sized pieces. If you want the chilli flavour but less heat, remove the seeds and leave them whole or cut them in half lengthways. How you cut the vegetables will depend on what you want to use it for: if it's for sandwiches, I chop everything pretty small and uniform; if it's to eat out of the jar as a snack or with charcuterie I leave everything pretty chunky, and keep the smaller florets whole.

Put the prepared vegetables in a large bowl with a few generous pinches of salt (you will rinse it after, so don't be shy). Give them a good mix and leave them to sit at room temperature for 1–2 hours. After this time, put the vegetables in a colander and rinse off the salt under cold running water. Set aside to drain.

Put the spices, bay leaves and chilli flakes in a large saucepan over a medium heat and lightly toast them for 2 minutes, then add the vinegar, water and sugar and bring to the boil. Add the drained vegetables and when the liquid returns to the boil, turn off the heat and leave it to steep. Once it's at room temperature, transfer the vegetables and pickling liquid to clean jars or containers and seal.

The pickle will keep for a year in the fridge and if you want to use sterilised jars it becomes shelf stable.

Pickled ginger deserves to be known as more than just something to have with sushi – it's a fantastic ingredient in itself and its pickling vinegar is just as useful. I often make this slaw when I'm eating something rich and spicy: for example, I almost always serve it with my Aubergine Parm (page 226) when I do dinner or supper clubs. It acts as a balancing palate cleanser while being fresh and crunchy.

fennel and pickled ginger slaw

SERVES 2–3

100ml neutral oil (I use rapeseed)
1 tsp fennel seeds
1 lemon
1 large fennel bulb (including fronds)
¼ head white cabbage
2 tbsp white wine vinegar
1 tbsp ginger pickling liquid
20g pickled ginger, finely chopped
salt

Put the oil and fennel seeds in a saucepan and place over a medium heat. Cook for 3–5 minutes until the seeds stop bubbling and turn light brown. Turn off the heat and leave to cool at room temperature.

Halve the lemon and have it ready to squeeze and rub over the fennel as you go (it keeps it from browning/oxidising). Pick all the fronds from the fennel – they taste more like fennel than any other part of the fennel other than the green stems, but the stems are too woody to eat raw – and set aside. Trim and discard the green part of the stems and halve the bulb lengthways. Rub some lemon over the bulb half you're not slicing first, then thinly slice the other half with a mandoline or a sharp knife and place in a bowl with the lemon juice, going on to slice the second half of the fennel and put it in the bowl. Thinly slice the cabbage with a mandoline or sharp knife as well, then mix with the fennel.

Add most of the fennel oil (saving a little for drizzling), vinegar, pickling liquid, chopped ginger and a good pinch of salt and mix well. Drizzle with the remaining fennel oil and seeds and garnish with the reserved fennel fronds.

There are almost always tomatoes in my kitchen, and more often than not they will be cherry tomatoes. If they are fresh and sweet, they get eaten like grapes or go in salads, and if they are a bit past their prime, used in sauces or made into pickles. I love having this pickle to hand – you can mix a few pickled tomatoes into a pasta sauce to give it some bite or add them to anything that could benefit from a sweet-sour pop of brightness. I love the texture of peeled tomatoes, but this still works with the skin on: just halve or quarter the tomatoes so the pickling liquid can do its thing.

pickled tomatoes

FILLS ONE 700ML OR TWO
350ML JARS OR CONTAINERS

300g cherry tomatoes
1 tsp black peppercorns
1 tsp fennel seeds
300ml water
200ml cider vinegar
100g caster sugar
1 tsp fine salt

Score a small cross on the bottom of each tomato. Place in a saucepan of boiling water for 30 seconds, then transfer to a bowl of iced water. The skin will have started to peel away where you made the score marks, making it easy to peel away the rest of the skin. Peel the skin from all the tomatoes and place them in a clean jar or container.

Lightly toast the fennel seeds and peppercorns in a DRY saucepan for 1–2 minutes over a medium heat, until fragrant, then add the water, vinegar and sugar and bring to the boil. Leave it to cool to room temperature then pour it over the peeled tomatoes. These are delicious after about 1 hour, but I normally leave them in the sealed jar or container at room temperature overnight. They keep in the fridge for a couple of weeks.

One of the best sandwiches I've ever had was made with aubergine and porchetta. I was in the Italian region of Puglia with my wife and kids a few years ago and the shop was an actual hole in the wall where a guy made fresh sandwiches and passed them out through a hatch. I asked for whatever he liked making the most, and he passed me the most perfectly simple sandwich – the aubergine was so good that I went back for a little bowl of it on its own. I love the combination of pickled or marinated vegetables with fatty meats – it's a flawless harmony and an easy way to elevate an otherwise basic meal. If you don't eat meat, put a handful of these on some Italian bread with burrata, shaved fennel and a couple of spoonfuls of the aubergine marinade, it's beautiful.

pickled and marinated aubergine

FILLS ONE 500ML JAR OR
CONTAINER

2 large aubergines
3 garlic cloves, 1 grated on a microplane grater, 2 thinly sliced
2 tsp fennel seeds
pared rind of 1 lemon
200ml olive oil, or a neutral oil like rapeseed (this volume of olive oil can be expensive)
3 tbsp white wine vinegar or white balsamic (I prefer white balsamic, but it can be expensive)
2 tsp dried chilli flakes
salt

Slice the aubergines into thin rounds (you can choose whether or not to peel them). Put them in a colander over a large bowl and sprinkle with a generous amount of salt. Mix well, then place a weight on top of the aubergine – a stack of plates will work. Leave at room temperature for 2–3 hours.

Put the sliced garlic cloves, fennel seeds and lemon rind in a saucepan with the olive oil. Cook over a low heat for 10 minutes, or until the garlic is lightly golden, then remove from the heat and leave to cool. I sometimes add a few chopped anchovy fillets (in oil) to this mix.

Squeeze out every last bit of moisture from the aubergine using your hands. Put it in a bowl with the vinegar, give it a good mix and leave for 5 minutes. Squeeze out the excess vinegar and put the aubergine in a clean jar with the dried chilli flakes, grated raw garlic, and the infused oil with all the aromatics. Give it a good mix and seal. This keeps for a couple weeks in the fridge or you can use a sterilised jar to store it for a long period of time.

For a good sandwich

I like to use an Italian sandwich bread called schiacciata romana, as my local deli has it, but any focaccia will do. If you can get or feel like making porchetta, go for it, but I usually use some prosciutto cotto or mortadella, adding the aubergine and its oil with some burrata and shaved fennel lightly dressed with a little salt and white wine vinegar or white balsamic. The balance is about 80/20 aubergine to ham and it's hard not to have it every week, so I do.

leafy

veg

and

salad

Tinned or jarred green lentils are always in my pantry and often end up in salads. Their texture really makes a salad into a meal for me, and when seasoned with Dijon mustard, lentils become very flavourful. Unless I'm making a ragout, I'll always use pre-cooked lentils. I love this with lardons, but it's still totally great without them – half my household prefers without, so I keep them separate and mix them through half the salad at the end.

spinach and lentil salad

SERVES **2**

50g smoked bacon lardons (optional)
30ml cider vinegar
20g capers, drained, plus 1 tbsp brine
15–20g Dijon mustard (I sometimes like to go for 30g)
1 tsp caster sugar (optional)
40ml extra virgin olive oil
½ shallot, finely diced
250g pre-cooked green lentils
1 large carrot, grated
100g spinach, rinsed and dried
handful of parsley, roughly chopped
handful of chives, finely chopped
juice of 1 lemon
salt and pepper

Put the lardons (if using) in a cold frying pan and place over a medium heat. Cook until all the fat has melted and the lardons are crispy, then transfer to paper towel to drain (I keep any rendered lardon/bacon fat from the pan in a sealed jar for another time).

Put the vinegar, caper brine, mustard and sugar (if using) in a large bowl with a damp towel underneath it (to help keep the bowl steady when you're whisking). Slowly stream in the oil, whisking continuously, until it's all combined, then stir in the shallot and set aside for 5 minutes. Bring the dressing back together with a whisk, then add the rest of the salad ingredients, reserving some herbs for garnish.

Make sure your hands are clean, then use them to mix the salad, breaking down the spinach a bit as you go. Check for seasoning and adjust it to your liking. Serve with lots of herbs on top and some fresh lemon on the side. It's a salad, so you can of course add things like tomatoes and cucumbers, but I try not to avoid overcrowding it.

I'm a big fan of charred lettuce. Charring a vegetable is such a simple way of changing the experience of the ingredient without losing its integrity. There is something deeply satisfying about burning a piece of lettuce –it sort of panics, and starts to crackle and burn, which is fun and exciting. Not normally words used when talking about lettuce. This combination is a rip on a Spanish classic, and the addition of artichokes gives a lot of body to the salad, making it superb for a light lunch. You can absolutely leave the anchovies out if you don't eat fish – the 'chokes go a long way.

grilled gem lettuce
with marinated artichokes

SERVES **2–3**

2 heads gem lettuce, halved
  lengthways
6 marinated artichokes
  (see page 79 or use
  shop-bought), halved or
  quartered
3 tbsp artichoke marinade,
  plus its aromatics (my
  recipe's aromatics include
  fennel seed, lemon rind,
  garlic, chilli)
1 tbsp sherry vinegar
½ banana shallot, finely diced
8 tinned anchovy fillets in oil
  (optional)
6 chives, finely chopped, to
  serve
salt and pepper

You can use a grill pan, barbecue or a grill rack over your gas hob to char the lettuce. You don't want to cook it, just get some good burn marks on it which add a ton of flavour – the lettuce should remain fresh and crunchy. Deeply char each piece over a high heat (just a minute on each side will do it) and then quarter it (cutting each grilled half in half again) so you have a balance of char and fresh on the exterior.

Mix the marinade, vinegar and shallot together to make the dressing and spoon it over the lettuce and 'chokes. I keep the anchovies whole so I can pick which bites I want to have them with. Garnish with chives and season with salt and pepper.

I was on holiday on the Sicilian island of Pantelleria a few years ago when I was tasked with making lunch for a group of friends, most of whom were fantastic cooks. I had forgotten to add the radicchio to an already dressed salad, so I quickly grilled it in a ripping-hot pan and made a sauce by blending a whole jar of capers and a tin of anchovies. It ended up getting a lot of appreciation and became one of my favourite things to eat – sometimes stress-cooking pays off.

grilled radicchio with caper and anchovy sauce

SERVES **4** AS A SIDE

100g tin anchovy fillets in oil
30g capers, drained
1 lemon, halved
4 tbsp extra virgin olive oil, plus extra to coat the radicchio
1 head purple radicchio
salt and pepper
handful of parsley, roughly chopped, to serve

First, make the sauce. Put the anchovies and oil, capers, the juice of half a lemon, and the olive oil in a blender and blend until smooth. If it's too thick, add a little water to loosen it.

Trim the radicchio stem, keeping the core intact, and remove any beaten-up outer leaves. Cut the radicchio into four pieces, then put it in a bowl with some olive oil to coat with a good pinch of salt and mix well.

Get a griddle pan or frying pan smoking hot over a high heat, then add the radicchio, cut side down, pressing it down firmly with your hand. Cook for 2 minutes, or until deeply charred. Turn the pieces and char them on the other cut side, then transfer to a plate. Squeeze the other half lemon over them while they steam.

You can put the sauce on the plate with the radicchio on top or spoon it over the radicchio. Finish with the chopped parsley and a little fresh cracked black pepper.

When I decided to change my career and focus on filming recipes, I knew I needed to get back into a professional kitchen. It had been over a decade since I'd worked in one and I was rusty. I called my friend, the brilliant chef Jackson Boxer, and before I had finished asking the question, he gave me a spot at one of his restaurants for a few nights a week. Cut to me in a corner of the kitchen being informed by the head chef that I was peeling carrots the wrong way and then taught how to do it right. That kitchen changed the direction of my life, and I'm forever grateful. That first night working a station I made about 50 of these salads and was thrilled by it. I loved stacking the leaves and covering the pile with finely grated cheese. This isn't Jackson's exact recipe but a loving nod to it.

a winter salad for jackson

SERVES 4 AS A SIDE

1 head Castelfranco
1 head endive
1 celery stalk, thinly sliced
   at an angle
10g chives, thinly sliced
120g walnut pieces, toasted
100g Comté cheese
salt

FOR THE DRESSING

3 tbsp cider vinegar
grated zest and juice of
   1 lemon
10g caster sugar or honey
1–2 tbsp Dijon mustard
100ml extra virgin olive oil

Trim the stems and separate the whole leaves of the Castelfranco and endive. Give them a good wash and dry before putting them in a big mixing bowl with the celery.

Put the vinegar, lemon juice and zest, sugar (or honey) and mustard in a mixing bowl. Slowly stream the oil in, whisking continuously – you want an emulsified dressing that has a good body to it, so it will coat the leaves.

Add the dressing to the leaves and celery with a good pinch of salt, mix, then add most of the chives and toasted nuts, reserving some of both for garnish. Gather the winter salad with both hands and gently set the leaves on your plate so they stay in a beautiful but imperfect pile. Add the remaining chives and nuts on top before grating the cheese over everything using a microplane grater.

If you don't eat fish, you can replace the tuna and anchovy with cooked white beans. This might feel like a side, but with the egg and fish or beans in the sauce, the body is there. It's got all the notes I love – creamy, bright, sour and sweet, with warming blistered vegetable goodness.

radicchio, tonnato and fried capers

SERVES 4

1 head purple radicchio, quartered
2 tbsp extra virgin olive oil
2 tbsp balsamic vinegar
1 tbsp capers, drained
flaky sea salt

FOR THE TONNATO

250g tin tuna in oil or 200g drained tinned or jarred butter beans
4 anchovy fillets in oil, drained
6 confit garlic cloves (see page 226)
1 egg, hard-boiled and cooled
2 tbsp extra virgin olive oil
juice of 1 lemon

Put the radicchio quarters in a bowl, add 1 tablespoon of the olive oil and some salt and use your hands to coat the radicchio with the oil. Heat a frying or griddle pan over a high heat, then place the radicchio quarters in the pan cut side down and sear until deeply charred – this happens quickly. Add a splash of water, cover and cook for 2–3 minutes. Transfer to a bowl while hot and dress with the balsamic vinegar. Leave to marinate while you make the tonnato.

Put the tuna (with its oil) and anchovies (or drained beans), confit garlic, boiled egg, olive oil and lemon juice in a food processor and blend until smooth, adding a bit more lemon juice if it becomes too thick. Check for seasoning – you will need salt if you opted for beans.

Dry the capers on a paper towel, then fry them in a frying pan over a medium heat for a minute or two until crisped up. Spread the tonnato over a plate. You can remove the core of the radicchio and separate the leaves or serve them in quarters – either way, add it to the tonnato with the balsamic vinegar and fried capers. I like to add a little flaky salt and another tablespoon of olive oil to serve.

I love the classic French/Belgian salad of endive, walnuts and blue cheese but as beautiful as it is with the whole endive leaves still intact, I never get as many bites as I would like that involve all the key players. This is why I make slaw – to get fully balanced and delicious mouthfuls from start to finish.

celery and endive slaw

SERVES 3–4

100g walnut halves
1 tbsp honey
1 tsp cayenne chilli powder
juice of ½ lemon
1 tbsp white wine vinegar
4 tbsp walnut oil or extra
  virgin olive oil
2 heads endive, halved
  lengthways, trimmed, and
  any battered outer leaves
  removed
3 celery stalks, thinly sliced
  at an angle, plus the leaves
handful of chives, thinly
  sliced
50g blue cheese, crumbled
salt and pepper

Preheat the oven to 180°C fan and line a baking sheet with baking paper.

Put the walnut halves in a bowl with the honey and give them a good mix. Sprinkle the cayenne and a generous pinch of salt over the nuts, making sure to get a little on each, then transfer to the lined baking sheet and bake for about 5 minutes, making sure to keep a close eye on them as they burn easily. Remove from the oven and leave to cool.

Put the lemon juice and vinegar into a mixing bowl with a good pinch of salt and some freshly cracked black pepper, then slowly stream the oil in while whisking continuously.

Thinly slice the endive and place in a large mixing bowl with the celery stalks and leaves, roasted walnuts, chives, and crumbled blue cheese, reserving some nuts, leaves, chives and cheese to garnish. Gently mix everything together with the dressing before serving.

The sauce I use here is inspired by nam jim jaew, a go-to Thai dipping sauce for meat, but I also love it with grilled vegetables, especially when they are deeply charred. I wanted to dress the entire dish with the sauce rather than use it as a dip, so I made it a bit lighter – no tamarind, a little less fish sauce – and added some lemongrass. If you don't eat meat, the fennel is great on its own.

fennel and steak with nam jim jaew-style sauce

SERVES 3–4

3 fennel bulbs (including fronds)
neutral oil, for drizzling
500g steak (I use bavette)
salt and pepper

FOR THE NAM JIM JAEW-STYLE SAUCE

10g dried rice (I use jasmine)
5g dried Thai chillies (or other dried chillies)
40ml lime juice
25ml fish sauce
1 lemongrass stalk, pounded, first layer peeled away, then minced
coriander stems from a handful of coriander, to taste
1 shallot, diced
15g palm sugar or caster sugar

Trim the fennel tops and reserve the fronds, then cut the bulbs into quarters. Lightly dress them with oil and season with salt, then cook under a hot grill, in a pizza oven, or on a barbecue. The sauce is punchy, so push the char on the fennel – the combination is delicious. You can cook the fennel to full tenderness if you prefer, but I like it to still have a little crunch.

Toast the uncooked rice in a hot, dry frying pan over a medium-high heat for 5–10 minutes, keeping it moving, until deeply browned, then blend in a spice grinder or grind by hand using a pestle and mortar, until finely ground. Toast the chillies in the same pan – they'll toast more quickly than the rice – and blend to flakes (or use shop-bought toasted chillies).

Mix the lime juice, fish sauce, rice powder, chilli flakes, lemongrass, coriander stems, plucked fennel fronds, shallot and sugar. Taste it, and if the lime juice/fish sauce is too strong, add a little bit more sugar – it should be sharp but balanced.

I like to add the fennel to the sauce while it's hot, but that does make it come out pretty intense, so lightly dressing it with the steak at the end will be more chill.

Cook the steak to your preferred doneness in a hot pan or on a grill, lightly oiling it and seasoning it with salt before putting it in the pan.

Serve the fennel with the steak and lots of black pepper.

Braising fennel intensifies its sweetness and mellows the aniseed. Braising also lets it keep its bite while simultaneously making it very tender. I often make this dish with Spanish chorizo in the chickpea mix, but the smoked paprika, chilli and garlic tell the same story if you're rolling without it. If you are, start by lightly frying it before you add the rest of the chickpea ingredients to the pan. I like to have this dish as a main.

braised fennel with spicy chickpeas and goat's curd

SERVES 2–3

2 fennel bulbs, trimmed and quartered
240ml dry white wine
240ml chicken or vegetable stock
2 tbsp unsalted butter
splash of white wine vinegar
2–3 tsp Dijon mustard
extra virgin olive oil, for drizzling
salt and pepper

FOR THE SPICY CHICKPEAS

100g Spanish chorizo, peeled and diced (optional)
1 tbsp olive oil
1 fresh chilli, finely chopped
2 garlic cloves, finely chopped
400g tin chickpeas, drained
1 tsp smoked paprika
splash of white wine vinegar
juice of 1 lemon

TO SERVE

½ bunch of chives, finely chopped
2 tbsp goat's curd

Coat the fennel quarters with olive oil and season them with salt. Sear them in a large hot frying pan over a medium heat for a few minutes until golden brown on both cut sides (this happens quickly). Deglaze the pan with the white wine and stock, cover and leave to cook for 10 minutes or until the fennel is tender.

In a separate frying pan, start preparing the spicy chickpeas. If you're using chorizo, fry it first: heat the olive oil in a frying pan over a medium heat, add the chorizo, and fry until crispy before adding the rest of the ingredients. Add the chilli, garlic and chickpeas and cook for a few minutes, then add the smoked paprika and cook for 1 minute. Add the vinegar and cook for 1–2 minutes, then remove from the heat and add the lemon juice, chives, and some salt and pepper.

When the fennel is tender, uncover the pan, add the butter, splash of vinegar and mustard to the braising liquid and mix until combined. Baste the fennel with the sauce as it thickens. I usually add a splash of water and some extra seasoning to stretch the sauce out before finishing.

Serve the braised fennel quarters topped with the spicy chickpeas and goat's curd.

When cooked, fennel becomes incredibly sweet and fragrant. Taking the time to make the jammy fennel and onion mix makes all the difference. This super-cosy meal has some fresh hits from the olive and sometimes I'll shave some fresh fennel very thinly and stir it through just before serving – this gives you the best of both worlds and really illustrates the impact that the cooking process has on the vegetable.

creamy beans with fennel and olives

SERVES **4**

2 fennel bulbs, including
  fronds if possible, plus extra
  raw fennel to serve (if you
  like)
juice of 1 lemon
1 white onion, thinly sliced
4 garlic cloves, thinly sliced
100ml olive oil
150ml dry white wine
70g green Spanish olives,
  drained, plus 1 tbsp brine
1 tbsp white miso paste
1 tbsp crème fraîche
700g jarred cannellini or
  butter beans, or 2 x 400g
  tins, drained (keep the
  liquid – the jarred one is
  best)
salt and pepper
crusty bread, to serve

Trim the green stalks of the fennel bulbs, reserving the fronds if present. Halve the bulbs lengthways, then cut them into 1cm-thick slices, coating the slices with a splash of lemon juice as you go (this prevents the fennel from oxidising and browning). Put the fennel, onion, garlic and olive oil in a casserole dish over a medium heat and cook for 20–30 minutes, until the fennel is soft and almost jammy, seasoning it with salt and pepper as it cooks.

Stir in the wine and cook for 5–10 minutes over a medium heat, then add the olives, olive brine, miso paste, crème fraîche and beans (and their jar liquid, if using), cook for a further 5 minutes then add the remaining lemon juice and serve garnished with the fennel fronds, some shaved raw fennel (if using), and some crusty bread.

It would never have occurred to me to eat cold noodles in broth with ice cubes, but when you do it, it instantly makes sense. Wait for an uncomfortably hot day and you will understand what this experience has to offer. Somyeon noodles are made with buckwheat, but any buckwheat noodle will work. Koreans eat this all year round but it's particularly good in the summer.

asparagus cold noodles with iced broth (korean-style naengmyeon)

SERVES 2–3

handful of asparagus spears, trimmed
2 x 40g single-serve packs instant dashi
400ml water
400g ice cubes, plus extra to serve
1 garlic clove, grated with a microplane grater
2–3 tsp light soy sauce
3 tbsp rice vinegar
1 cucumber
200g cherry tomatoes
2 tbsp caster sugar
200g somyeon noodles (soba noodles or other buckwheat noodles will do)
1 tsp English mustard
1 tsp toasted sesame oil
2 spring onions, trimmed and thinly sliced
2–3 radishes, thinly sliced
white sesame seeds, toasted, to serve

Blanch the asparagus in salted boiling water for 2–3 minutes, then remove and refresh in iced water or under a cold tap. Drain, slice in half lengthways and set aside.

Make the dashi with 200ml of the water in a saucepan over a medium heat, following the packet instructions. Once it has dissolved, turn off the heat and add the remaining 200ml water and the ice. This speeds the cooling. Once cooled, add the grated garlic, soy sauce and vinegar.

Julienne the cucumber (cut it into thin strips) or use a box grater to slice it, grating at a steep angle to get the longest strips possible. Quarter the tomatoes and put them into a bowl with the cucumber and asparagus. Add a good pinch of salt and the sugar, mix well and set aside.

Cook the noodles according to the packet instructions, then rinse in a sieve or colander under a cold running tap to stop them cooking.

Divide between bowls, add the noodles, a handful of ice cubes, English mustard, sesame oil, spring onions, radishes and sesame seeds.

The first restaurant I worked in was an Italian-American spot in an outdoor mall in the San Fernando Valley. I was a busboy and committed the cardinal sin of popping a prepped ingredient in my mouth as I walked past one of the chef's stations. I rightly got my head absolutely ripped off. I was later forgiven, and it ended up being somewhere I loved working and where I learned a lot about food. One of the stations had a huge pan of beautiful pale-yellow liquid that would get ladled onto dishes, an emulsion of lemon juice, clarified butter and a little garlic. It was – for lack of a better word – the BEST! Most days I'd have it alone with pasta. It's a great way to finish dishes and it goes very well with this classic spring vegetable dish, adding a little acidic brightness and body.

asparagus, rice and lemon butter

SERVES 3

2 handfuls asparagus spears, trimmed and each cut into three (don't discard the woody ends)
900ml water
100ml dry white wine (or just use more asparagus stock if you prefer)
200g unsalted butter or clarified butter (I use clarified if I have it, but it's not necessary)
2 garlic cloves, peeled and bashed
grated zest and juice of 2 lemons
2 tbsp extra virgin olive oil
1 small brown onion, finely diced or grated
175g risotto rice
100g podded broad beans or peas (frozen are great)
12 chives, finely chopped
salt and pepper

Put the cleaned woody ends of the spears in a saucepan with the water, bring to the boil, then reduce the heat and simmer for 10–20 minutes. Add the white wine and bring it back to a simmer – this will be our stock for cooking the rice. I season the stock with salt until it tastes... nice. Then I know my rice will also have a similar seasoning with a little adjustment at the end.

Put the butter, bashed garlic and most of the lemon zest into a saucepan and place over a low heat. Once the butter has melted, allow it to slowly warm for 10 minutes, then turn off the heat and add the lemon juice. Blend until everything is broken down and the sauce is emulsified. Pass it through a sieve to get rid of the lemon zest and any pieces of garlic, then set aside in a warm spot (you can use a whisk or stick blender to bring it back together with a splash of stock or water if the emulsion breaks).

Put the olive oil and diced or grated onion into a large sauté pan, place over a low heat and cook slowly until softened for 5–10 minutes, avoiding any browning. Turn the heat up to medium and add the rice, stirring it through the onion for about a minute. Now gradually start adding the warm stock, 2–3 ladles at a time, stirring often and adding more once the liquid has almost all been absorbed by the rice. Stop when the rice is tender with a little bite. Add the broad beans or peas and the asparagus pieces, cook for 2–3 minutes until they are just softened, then stir through a few generous spoons of the lemon butter. There should be enough liquid to run on the bottom of the pan – if it's thick, add a little stock to loosen it.

Finish with black pepper, the rest of the lemon zest and the chives.

Asparagus with hollandaise is a classic and this a super fun way of enjoying those beloved flavours. You can also just go full mixed vegetable tempura here – the combination of light airy batter, sweet vegetables and rich sauce is truly a beautiful thing.

I love making tempura for parties as people can crowd around the stove and eat as you cook. When cooking requires a balance of total precision and lawlessness, I'm in my happy place. Keeping the batter the right temperature and consistency, cleaning the oil as you go, but also covering your bare hand in the batter and drizzling it into the hot oil from a height, you enter a truly transformative cooking zone – wizard monk vibes.

Tempura can be tricky to perfect but you're at home and having fun, so leave that stress to the professionals. If you can get your hands on cake flour, I've found that makes a big difference, but plain flour works too.

The key things are to use a good amount of ice in the batter and cold water, to avoid overmixing it – lumps are okay – and to keep it thin (it should just coat your hand, and should have a consistency like crêpe batter).

asparagus tempura with yuzu hollandaise

SERVES **4** FOR SHARING

1 quantity Hollandaise (see
  page 163)
1–2 tbsp yuzu juice (to taste)
24 asparagus spears, trimmed
200g cake flour or plain flour,
  plus a little extra for dusting
30g cornflour
400ml cold water
a few ice cubes
neutral oil, for deep-frying
  (I use rapeseed)
shichimi togarashi, to taste
salt

Follow the hollandaise recipe on page 163, substituting the fresh lemon juice with yuzu juice.

You can blanch and refresh the asparagus in salted water before frying or fry it from raw. The only benefit of the blanching is getting a bit of seasoning in the spears before you fry them but it's good both ways.

Sift the flour into a large bowl then whisk in the cornflour. Add the cold water and mix with a wooden spoon, never stirring too fast. It will be very lumpy at first and will slowly break down. Pea-sized lumps are cool – you can use your fingers to break down any bigger lumps. Add the ice when it's looking good.

Heat the oil for deep-frying in a casserole dish or any large, tall pan over a medium heat until it reaches 170–180°C.

Lightly dust the asparagus spears in flour, then dip them in the batter. This is where you have to move fast, transferring the spears from batter to oil in one move, drawing a circle with the spear as you lay it gently in the oil and letting any excess batter fall from your fingers over the top as it fries. I usually dip my hand in the batter and drizzle a little extra into the oil while the asparagus is frying, so it has crispy goodness on top.

Fry the spears in batches of 4–6 at a time. Remove carefully with metal tongs and leave to drain on a wire rack, seasoning them with salt while they are still hot. Use a small sieve or slotted spoon to clean the excess batter out of the oil between batches. This saves overcooked batter covering your next batch.

Sprinkle the hollandaise with togarashi, to taste, and dip the crispy spears into it.

Marinated artichokes are a really useful thing to have in your fridge and are very easy to make with artichoke hearts from a tin. Mixed with some feta cheese and tomato and served on top of toast, they make a simple but delicious weekday lunch, or try throwing them into a salad or onto your next pizza to make the whole thing more interesting. One of my favourite ways to eat marinated artichokes is in a pasta salad with capers, olives, anchovies, herbs, feta, good olive oil and a load of red wine vinegar. I generally make them pretty spicy and fragrant, but you can add whatever aromatics you prefer.

marinated artichokes

MAKES **800**G

2 x 400g tins artichoke hearts in water, drained
pared rind and juice of 1 lemon
4 tbsp white wine vinegar
150ml extra virgin olive oil
1 fresh jalapeño chilli, cut into julienne (thin strips)
1 tbsp dried chilli flakes
1 tsp fennel seeds
4 garlic cloves, thinly sliced
2 thyme sprigs
salt and pepper

Cut the drained artichoke hearts into your desired shape – bite-sized chunks or quarters work well – and place in a heatproof bowl, then add the lemon juice, vinegar, some fresh cracked black pepper and a good pinch of salt. Leave to sit while you prepare the oil.

Put the oil in a saucepan with the red chilli, chilli flakes, fennel seeds, strips of lemon rind, garlic and thyme sprigs. Place over a medium-low heat and cook for 5–8 minutes or until the garlic very slightly starts to brown. Pour the oil over the artichoke hearts, mix well and allow it to cool. They will keep in the fridge, covered, for about 2 weeks.

My mom grew up in a small town in Illinois where her dad grew vegetables in his free time, so she learned from an early age how to make the most of them in the kitchen. I remember the first time she prepared artichokes for me and my siblings, serving a steaming pile of them with a bowl of mayonnaise and fresh lemon. We ended up fighting over the heart when we got to it. I come back to this experience often when I'm thinking of recipes: a group of LA city kids who loved fast food devouring a pile of vegetables. I love food that makes you use your hands. Plucking the warm leaves and scraping the tender flesh with your teeth is deeply satisfying. If I were serving them for dinner it could be alongside grilled/baked white fish with lots of lemon and capers, but we often have them with a few pieces of sourdough bread and a simple tomato salad with lots of nice olive oil and balsamic. If you don't like mayonnaise, make lemon butter (French vinaigrette is also common and delicious). I love shop-bought mayo but if I'm going to have it stand on its own two feet at the table then I'm making it. It's a great skill to have in the kitchen and incredibly satisfying to see it come together.

Artichokes can be intimidating, and processing them can test the patience of any cook, but this is one the easiest ways to prepare and enjoy a 'choke.

Globe artichokes usually start to pop up in supermarkets when they are good and in season: they should have a nice colour (purple or green) and tight squeaky leaves. The cooking time will vary from 20 to 60 minutes according to their size – I prefer larger ones as you get more flesh on the leaves. You will need a relatively big stock pot.

continued overleaf...

artichokes with homemade mayonnaise and fresh lemon

SERVES **2** AS A MAIN OR **4–5** AS
A STARTER

2–3 large globe artichokes
3–4 lemons (I like to use a
lot), washed and halved

FOR THE MAYONNAISE

1 egg yolk
1 tsp Dijon mustard
350ml rapeseed oil
1 tbsp lemon juice
1 tbsp white wine vinegar
sea salt/table salt, to taste

For the mayonnaise you can use any oil that you prefer – just be aware that the finished mayo will taste very strongly of that oil. Rapeseed is essentially flavourless, and will result in something that echoes what you buy in the shops.

Use a medium-large mixing bowl. Dampen a tea towel, roll it up and curl it into the shape of a coiled snake on your work surface. This will keep your bowl in place while you work. Start by whisking the egg yolk and mustard. When they are combined, start slowly dripping in the oil, whisking continuously. When it starts to thicken, add a squeeze of lemon juice to loosen the mixture. Continue adding oil and repeat the process, alternating between adding lemon juice and vinegar, until the mayo reaches your desired consistency. Taste and season with salt. There is almost no limit to how much oil you can add, so just stop when you're happy.

Trim the stems of the artichokes to the base. This should make them flat enough to be able to sit upright. Put the halved lemons in a large pan of water with a few good pinches (3 finger pinches) of salt. Add the artichokes, bring to the boil, cover and cook for anything from 20–60 minutes, depending on the size of your artichokes. Remove when you can pull a leaf away with little to no resistance. Let them sit on a tea towel and release some steam for a few minutes. Eat the flesh from the leaves until they become so small that it's no longer worth the effort. Remove the rest, then carefully scrape the hairs from the heart. Enjoy your prize – the most vegetable-tasting of vegetables.

This is one of the first things I make when asparagus comes into season. The combination of sweet and crunchy asparagus with tender lamb, brought together by fresh punchy mint, is a celebration of spring and the bounty it has to offer. You could make this with grilled asparagus instead, but I opt for the blanching method as it really lets the flavour sing and gives a good contrast to the char of the lamb.

Swap the meat for a soft-boiled or poached egg if you like.

asparagus, peas and mint with lamb

SERVES **2**

8–10 asparagus spears, trimmed
4 tbsp frozen peas
250g lamb rump
2 heads baby gem lettuce, halved lengthways
handful of mint leaves
handful of parsley, roughly chopped
handful of chives, finely chopped
salt and pepper

FOR THE DRESSING

1 tbsp Dijon mustard
3 tbsp extra virgin olive oil
2 tbsp white wine vinegar
juice of ½ lemon
1 small banana shallot, finely chopped
1 tsp caster sugar

Mix the dressing ingredients together in a bowl, season with salt and pepper, and leave to sit at room temperature while you prepare the rest of the meal. This will take the edge off the shallot.

Preheat the oven to 200°C fan.

Blanch the asparagus and peas in salted boiling water for 3 minutes, then transfer to an ice bath. The briefer the blanching time, the more heavily you want to season the water (if I'm blanching a vegetable under 5 minutes, I heavily salt the water so it's like sea water). Remove once cool and pat dry. Halve lengthways at an angle.

Cook the lamb in an ovenproof frying pan fat side down over a medium-high heat until it develops a good colour – about 5 minutes – then flip and transfer to the oven and roast for 10–12 minutes. If you don't have an ovenproof pan, transfer the lamb to a baking tray that has been heated up in the oven. The internal temperature of the lamb should be 55–60°C on a temperature probe – it will go up to 60–65°C while it rests. This gives you nice medium rare doneness. Remove from the pan and set aside to rest.

Char the lettuce halves, cut side down, in a smoking-hot grill pan (just a minute or so will do it).

When the lamb has cooled to room temperature, thinly slice it then combine it with the charred lettuce, peas, *asparagus*, mint, parsley and chives. Add the dressing and lots of fresh cracked black pepper.

I don't think I've ever met someone who loves to cook that doesn't love eating and making artichokes à la Barigoule. Processing an artichoke for its heart can feel for me like dancing, then fighting, and it honestly even makes me meditate on my own mortality. You have to be brutal and that brutality will be rewarded. This recipe stays pretty close to the classic, with a little extra lemon and a combination of stock and wine.

braised purple artichokes

SERVES 2–3

8–10 small purple artichokes
3 tbsp extra virgin olive oil
1 shallot, diced
2 carrots, cut at an angle into uneven bite-sized pieces
2 garlic cloves, bashed
3 thyme sprigs
1 bay leaf
150ml dry white wine
150ml vegetable stock or water
20g unsalted butter
juice of 1 lemon
handful of parsley, roughly chopped
salt and pepper

Cut the dark woody leaves from the top of the artichokes and peel away the bottom of the leaves until they are pale yellow with a faint purple hue at the top. Keep dipping them in a bowl of water with lemon juice added as you go, to prevent them oxidising. Use a vegetable peeler to peel the stem and trim around the edges till only pale flesh remains. You can use a spoon to dig out the hairy choke if you want to keep them whole, or slice them in half lengthways – slicing them in half will make it easier to remove the choke. Let them soak in the lemon water until you're ready to cook.

Put the oil, shallot, carrot, garlic, thyme, bay leaf, artichokes, and a pinch each of salt and pepper in a large saucepan (that you have a lid for) and place over a medium heat. Cook for 1–2 minutes, then add the wine and stock or water. Bring to the boil, then reduce the heat and simmer, covered with a lid, for 10 minutes. Keep an eye on it – if the liquid burns off too quickly, add a bit more stock as you go.

Turn off the heat, remove the herbs and garlic, and finish the sauce, adding the butter, lemon juice and parsley and stirring gently with a wooden spoon until it's emulsified. Transfer to a plate and serve.

I rarely see this classic Belgian dish in restaurants or cookbooks. It has a great balance of bitter, sweet and richness from the butter and is often served as a side, but the addition of goat's curd helps make it substantial enough for a light lunch.

butter-braised endive

SERVES 2–3

4 Belgian endives, halved
2 tbsp unsalted butter
120ml dry white wine or
  chicken stock
2 garlic cloves, thinly sliced
  or grated
1 tbsp white wine vinegar
1½ tsp sugar or honey
juice of ½ lemon
2 tbsp goat's curd, or labneh
  or thick Greek yoghurt
  seasoned with salt and
  lemon juice
1–2 tsp white miso paste
handful of chives, thinly
  sliced
salt

Lightly sear the endive halves cut side down in a frying pan with the butter over a medium heat. They have a tendency to stick – adding a little salt to the pan before you add the endive will help prevent this. You're aiming for deep colour and caramelisation, but it's best to take your time getting there so they don't burn; they'll take about 5 minutes. Once caramelised, flip the endive halves over, season with salt and add the wine or stock. Cover with a lid and simmer over a low heat for 6–7 minutes until the wine (or stock) has almost all evaporated. Remove the lid and add the garlic, vinegar, and the sugar or honey. This balances the bitterness of the endive. Cook for a few more minutes over a medium heat.

Remove the endive halves from the pan and add the lemon juice, a little water and the white miso (start with 1 teaspoon, then add more if you like) to the pan. Mix well and cook over a medium heat for a minute or two until you have a smooth pan sauce. Spoon this over the endive.

Add a few spoons of goat's curd or yoghurt, and some chives, then serve.

There is a basic formula I follow when making a salad dressing – oil, vinegar, salt and a little sugar for balance. Using that formula offers endless possibilities; I usually end up making a French-style mustard vinaigrette or a Japanese carrot and ginger dressing. They both work well with whatever lettuce or raw vegetables you use. They have a bright refreshing presence that offers balance to a meal without distracting from the flavours. They also have the ability to make simple weeknight dishes feel like a meal.

For the salad, I use butterhead lettuce with shallot, spring onion or chives. I love the texture of butterhead, and that you can present it as a whole head. You wash it whole, then remove the core before letting it spread out like an open flower on a large plate.

same salad, different dressing

MAKES 250ML (8–10 SERVINGS)

CARROT AND GINGER DRESSING

1 medium carrot, peeled
2.5cm piece of ginger, peeled
¼ medium white onion
1 garlic clove (optional)
25ml toasted sesame oil
100ml neutral oil (I use
   rapeseed)
100ml rice vinegar (or any
   white vinegar)
1 tsp light soy sauce
1 tbsp sweet white miso
   paste (this is sweeter than
   standard white miso)
5–10g caster sugar

Blend all the ingredients in a
blender until smooth.

MAKES 200ML (6–8 SERVINGS)

DIJON VINAIGRETTE

100ml extra virgin olive oil
50ml white wine vinegar
50g Dijon mustard
5–10g sugar or honey
salt and pepper

Whisk all the ingredients
together until smooth and
season to taste with salt
and pepper.

tomatoes

peppers

courgettes

cucumbers

Confit refers to the process of slow cooking and storing food in fat and it is a great way to extract deep flavour and get luscious texture, especially from vegetables. The oil can be strained afterwards and used for vinaigrettes and sauces. It might seem like a scarily technical process because of the name but it's really as simple as it gets. Using this process to make tomato soup is dreamy – with confit you get the same sorts of benefits you do from roasting vegetables, without the deeper darker browning notes, and you also get a delicious infused oil to blend through the soup, as well as drizzle.

confit tomato soup with parmesan and sesame crisp

SERVES **4–6**

500g cherry tomatoes on the vine
1 fresh red chilli
6 garlic cloves, peeled but left whole
1 celery stalk, chopped
1 shallot, peeled and halved
1 thyme sprig
neutral oil (I use rapeseed), to cover
130g tube of tomato pureé (triple-concentrated is best here)
500ml vegetable stock or water
1 tsp red wine vinegar (optional)
1 tsp caster sugar (optional)
salt and pepper
crème fraîche, to serve
chopped chives, to serve

FOR THE PARMESAN AND SESAME CRISP (OPTIONAL)

100g Parmesan cheese, finely grated with a microplane grater
1 heaped tbsp mixed sesame seeds

Put the tomatoes (with their stems) in a medium saucepan with the chilli, garlic, celery, shallot and thyme, then add enough oil to just cover. Cook over a low heat for 30 minutes. It should lightly bubble away, never fry, and only start to become lightly browned towards the end of cooking.

Strain the oil (it will keep at room temperature in a sealed jar) and remove the stems from the tomatoes and the thyme sprig. Add the tomato mixture to a blender with a spoonful of the confit oil and a few spoonfuls of water and blend for at least 1 minute on high speed until completely smooth. If it's thick, add a few spoonfuls of water and blend until it runs smoothly.

Put a few spoonfuls of the confit oil into a saucepan with the tomato pureé and fry over a medium-high heat for about 5 minutes. It should caramelise slightly and smell very sweet and fragrant. Add the confit tomato mix, stock or water and some salt and pepper. Mix well and simmer for 10 minutes.

While the soup simmers, make the crisp. Preheat the oven to 180°C fan and line a baking sheet with baking paper. Put 4–6 piles of grated Parmesan on the lined sheet and bake in the oven for 7–10 minutes, sprinkling over the sesame seeds when the cheese starts to melt. When the cheese starts to lightly colour, remove from the oven and remove the pieces of crisp from the baking sheet with a spatula while warm.

I like to season my soup with vinegar and a little sugar but it's optional.

Serve the soup in bowls, with the crisp cracked over the soup and a dollop of crème fraîche and chopped chives.

TOMATOES PEPPERS COURGETTES CUCUMBERS

What I crave most in a butter chicken is the rich, creamy and fragrant tomato sauce. This recipe is my way of doubling down on that flavour and seeing how far I can take it. I know it can be a bit 'cheffy' to layer the same ingredient multiple times in a dish, but it works really well here without requiring much effort (now you're used to me having you peel your tomatoes). Spending time in India I learned very quickly that ingredients, techniques and flavours change from one town to the next – recipes are not written in stone, so it is okay to take inspiration from a dish and make it your own. I like this blend of spices but if you feel like something isn't right, do you. Serve with hot flatbread or rice.

butter tomato

SERVES 3–4

4 tbsp neutral oil (I use rapeseed)
2 red onions, thinly sliced
6 large tomatoes, peeled and quartered
4 garlic cloves, finely chopped
handful of coriander, leaves and stems
thumb-sized piece of ginger, finely chopped
4 tbsp unsalted butter
130g double-concentrated tomato purée
2 tbsp rice vinegar
100ml chicken stock, vegetable stock or water
250ml double cream
225g paneer, cubed
500g cherry tomatoes, peeled if you wish (see page 51), and left whole or halved

FOR THE SPICES

1 cinnamon stick
4 cloves
2 bay leaves
6 black peppercorns
2 green cardamom pods
2 black cardamom pods
1–2 tsp deggi mirch (or other chilli powder)
1 tbsp ground coriander

FOR THE GHEE TOPPING (OPTIONAL)

2 tbsp ghee
1 tbsp cumin seeds
1 dried chilli
1 tsp Kashmiri chilli powder (or any chilli powder)

continued overleaf...

butter tomato *(continued)*

Put the oil, red onions, quartered tomatoes, garlic, coriander stems, ginger and all the spices in a large saucepan over a high heat and sauté for 2–3 minutes, stirring continuously. Reduce the heat, cover with a lid, and simmer for 10 minutes.

Remove the cinnamon stick and blend the tomato and onion mix at high speed for at least 1–2 minutes until smooth, then strain and discard the residue. Set aside.

Put the butter, tomato purée, vinegar and stock or water in a pan large enough for the curry. Cook over a medium-high heat for 3–4 minutes, stirring continuously, until the liquid has reduced and formed a thick paste. Add the cream and continue to cook for 5–10 minutes, stirring, until you have a thick, glossy sauce. Stir in the strained tomato and onion mix, then add the paneer and simmer for 5 minutes. Add the cherry tomatoes and cook for just long enough to warm them through (about 1 minute).

There is oil, butter and cream here, so I'd understand if you wanted to skip the ghee topping, but I never do. Heat the ghee in a small frying pan over a medium heat, then add the spices and mix briefly until fragrant. Spoon the spiced ghee over the curry and serve the curry with hot flatbread or rice.

Sweet tomatoes, smoky peppers and salty creamy cheese – this is one of my go-tos for summer meals. I really think taking the time to peel the tomatoes makes a big difference: once you become a peeled tomato person it's pretty hard to look back. I like to grab a good mix of tomatoes, varying shape, size and colour; it looks beautiful and is nice to have a variety of textures and flavours.

tomato and marinated pepper tart

SERVES 6

100g double-concentrate tomato purée
6 tinned anchovy fillets in oil (optional)
1 garlic clove, grated on a microplane grater
2 tbsp extra virgin olive oil, plus extra for drizzling
800g mixed tomatoes
1 tbsp sherry vinegar
300g marinated roasted/ grilled red peppers from a jar
250g ricotta cheese
1 sheet shop-bought puff pastry (320g)
1 egg, beaten
1 tsp dried red chilli flakes
handful of parsley
handful of basil
salt and pepper

Preheat the oven to 180°C fan.

Put the tomato purée, anchovies (if using) and grated garlic in a saucepan with the olive oil and fry over a medium-high heat for 2–3 minutes, stirring continuously. Transfer to a bowl and leave to cool.

Score, blanch and refresh the tomatoes: cut a small cross on the top of each tomato, put them in boiling water for 30 seconds, then transfer to an ice bath. Peel and cut into uneven pieces, keeping the cherry tomatoes whole. Put into a bowl with a pinch of salt, another 2 tablespoons of olive oil and the sherry vinegar. Slice the peppers in half lengthways and add them to the bowl.

Whisk the ricotta and fried tomato purée in a bowl.

Roll out the puff pastry onto a baking sheet, keeping it on the paper it comes rolled up in, and lightly score a 2.5cm border around the edge. Brush beaten egg around the border, then spread the ricotta mixture evenly over the rest of the pastry. Layer the peppers and tomatoes over the top and bake in the oven for 25–30 minutes, until the puff pastry is puffy and golden at the edges and everything's looking good.

Remove from the oven and serve garnished with the chilli flakes, some torn parsley and basil, a sprinkle of pepper and a little drizzle of olive oil.

TOMATOES PEPPERS COURGETTES CUCUMBERS

Having good condiments to hand is essential for a happy life. Furikake (a Japanese dried seasoning blend made with seaweed and sesame seeds) is always in my pantry – there are several varieties and although they are all universally good with rice, I use different flavours for certain dishes. I've used nori tamago (seaweed egg) flavour for this salad. If you haven't tried it, give it a go. I literally said, 'f*** yeah' out loud when I tasted this for the first time.

tomato and furikake pasta salad

SERVES **3–4**

500g tomatoes (anything that tastes good)
pinch of caster sugar
300g dried pasta (I often use elbow or fusilli)
6 spring onions, green part only, thinly sliced at an angle
½ cucumber, sliced and quartered
100g mayonnaise
20ml rice vinegar
1 tbsp capers
1 tbsp furikake
salt (optional)
coriander sprigs, to garnish

Cut the tomatoes into uneven large bite-sized pieces, then season with some salt and the pinch of sugar. Mix well and set aside at room temperature while you cook the pasta.

Cook the pasta in salted boiling water according to the packet instructions, then drain and rinse in a colander under cold running water until cool. Once cooled, leave to drain for a few minutes – you want it as dry as possible.

Combine the rest of the ingredients with the pasta, reserving half the furikake and green spring onion for the garnish. Everything is salty here, so there probably won't be a need for any additional salt. Top with coriander sprigs.

I'm one of those people who finds a song they like and listens to it on a loop for the entire day and I'll often do the same with food. While writing this book, I ordered tom kha kai six nights in a row. I've had it countless times, but for some reason it hit me like the first time I tried it and I kept going back. It always comes with mushrooms, and annoyingly I can't eat them any more (although they are still in this book for you), so I would add an entire punnet of peeled cherry tomatoes instead and it was totally delicious. I wanted to make something that really leaned into that combination and this is what I came up with: a Tom Kha Tomato soup, baby.

tomato tom kha

SERVES **4**

250g cherry tomatoes
1 tbsp palm sugar or light brown sugar, or to taste (plus a pinch for the tomatoes)
2 tbsp fish sauce (plus a little for the tomatoes)
400g tin full-fat coconut milk, chilled
150g double-concentrated tomato purée
1 litre chicken stock
100g fresh oyster mushrooms, halved (keep some whole if you like)
thumb-sized piece of galangal, cut into 1cm-thick discs
2 lemongrass stalks, peeled, smashed and roughly chopped into thirds
6 lime leaves
400g tin evaporated milk
1 tbsp Thai chilli jam
handful of coriander, leaves and stems, roughly chopped
juice of 2 limes

If you want to keep the skin on the tomatoes it's all good, I'm just a peeled tomato guy. To peel, score a small cross in each tomato and boil it for 30 seconds, then transfer to an ice bath. Peel the skin and transfer to a bowl with a little fish sauce and a pinch of sugar, mix and set aside at room temperature while you prepare the soup.

I use the coconut cream to fry the tomato purée, so you will need to separate it (I chill my coconut milk tin in advance so that I can separate the coconut cream). Put the cream that has solidified at the top of the tin and the tomato purée in a large saucepan, place over a medium heat, and fry for about 5 minutes until thick and fragrant. Add the stock, mushrooms, 1 tablespoon of the fish sauce, the galangal, lemongrass, lime leaves and a pinch of salt, then bring to a simmer, stirring gently in one direction (this keeps the coconut milk from separating), for 10 minutes. Add the evaporated milk, coconut milk, chilli jam, and the remaining fish sauce and sugar, then simmer, stirring gently in 1 direction again, for another 10 minutes. Add the tomatoes, coriander and lime juice just before serving. Check for seasoning and send it in the direction you like.

I often have it with Thai red rice or jasmine rice.

Everyone should have a go-to tomato sauce. This is mine. Garlic and chilli bubbling in golden oil until almost brown, then arrested by tinned tomatoes, steaming and spitting in the hot oil. A little salt and a splash of sweet vinegar and you have a sauce that will confidently tell anyone to sit down, be quiet, and eat.

arrabbiata

SERVES **2**

400g tin peeled plum
  tomatoes
100ml extra virgin olive oil
6 garlic cloves, thinly sliced
1 tsp dried red chilli flakes
100g tomato purée
1 tbsp white wine vinegar
1 tsp caster sugar
200g dried spaghetti
salt and pepper

Tip the tinned tomatoes into a large bowl and use your hands to crush them, leaving some texture with no real uniformity.

Heat the oil in a saucepan over a medium heat and add the sliced garlic and chilli flakes. Fry until the garlic starts to take on a little colour, then add the tomato purée. Fry for 2–3 minutes, allowing the purée to caramelise and stick to the pan a little, stirring continuously. Add the crushed tinned tomatoes, give it a good stir, then allow the sauce to bubble away over a medium-low heat for 10 minutes. Add the vinegar, sugar and some salt, then cook for another 2–3 minutes. Set aside.

Cook the spaghetti in a large pot of seasoned boiling water till al dente. Transfer the spaghetti straight from the water to the pan of sauce, along with a few spoonfuls of the pasta cooking water. Finish over a medium heat for about 1–2 minutes until everyone is getting along. Serve with a little freshly cracked black pepper.

TOMATOES PEPPERS COURGETTES CUCUMBERS

One of my favourite parts of an al pastor taco is the small pieces of pineapple that get thrown in which are sweet and a little tender, and take on the flavour of the pork. A pineapple taco is also very good alone and, when I make them at home, I'll grill enough to have a one-to-one balance of pineapple tacos to meat tacos. You want to use an unripe pineapple for this, so it doesn't fall apart – it literally has to be as hard as a rock.

grilled pineapple tacos

SERVES **4–6**

1 unripe pineapple, peeled and cored, flesh cut into large planks (keep the core and dice it for a salsa if you don't want to waste it)
6 limes
neutral oil (I use rapeseed), for drizzling
100g tinned chipotles in adobo
4 tbsp tahini
1 tbsp white vinegar
½ head white cabbage
4–6 corn tortillas
bunch of coriander, roughly chopped
1 white onion, diced
200g feta cheese, crumbled
salt and pepper

Season the pineapple with salt and pepper and the juice of 2 of the limes, and drizzle with a little of the oil. Mix well and set aside.

Put the chipotles, tahini, vinegar and the juice of 2 of the limes in a blender and blitz until smooth. Add a little water if it gets too thick, and check for seasoning. Set aside.

Cut the cabbage as thinly as possible – I use a mandoline.

Grill the seasoned pineapple planks on a smoking-hot barbecue grill or griddle pan for a couple of minutes until deeply charred on all sides. When they are ready, keep them warm in the pan over a low heat.

Warm the tortillas over an open flame or in a hot dry frying pan, until soft and pliable.

To make the tacos, add the sauce to a warm tortilla, followed by a little shredded cabbage, and some pineapple. Finish with some coriander, diced onion, crumbled feta and a squeeze of fresh lime.

I can eat stuffed dates like I'm being paid to do it. My favourites are stuffed with blue cheese and jalapeños, and are often wrapped in bacon. This is my way of turning the experience into a kind-of meal of sweet, spicy and savoury goodness.

date, stilton and jalapeño puff pastry

SERVES 6

1 small Maris Piper potato (peeled if you like), very thinly sliced using a mandoline
200g Stilton, roughly crumbled
50g ricotta cheese
2 spring onions, white parts thinly sliced, green parts reserved for garnish
3 fresh jalapeño chillies, thinly sliced
1 sheet shop-bought puff pastry (320g)
1 egg, beaten
150g pitted dates, roughly chopped
1 tbsp olive oil
flaky salt and black pepper

Preheat the oven to 180°C fan.

Par-cook the sliced potato in salted boiling water for 3 minutes, then drain and leave to dry on a clean tea towel.

In a bowl, mix the Stilton, ricotta, white part of the spring onion and sliced jalapeños.

Unroll the puff pastry on its paper on an oven tray and lightly score a 2.5cm line around the edge – this allows the pastry at the edge to rise, giving you a crust. Brush beaten egg around the border, then spread the cheese mixture evenly over the rest of the pastry. Layer the potato slices over the cheese and scatter over the dates, then drizzle with the olive oil and grind over some black pepper. Bake in the oven for 25–30 minutes, until the pastry is puffy and golden.

Eat it warm, garnished with the green part of the spring onion.

I have been known to add some hot honey to this one while eating.

Courgettes are abundant and versatile, so I use them as much as I can. When they are shaved into long strips, they look beautiful and create an amazing texture for salads. This is one of the easiest salads for making a meal feel special, and it's on our table throughout the summer – whether we're having a barbecue or eating pasta, it balances everything out. You can add different whole herbs to marry it with your meal: for example, dill and mint are amazing when the salad is paired with heavily spiced grilled lamb. This version is stripped back with all the focus on the courgette's sweet and delicate flavour.

shaved courgette salad

SERVES 6

4 courgettes
100ml extra virgin olive oil
juice of 1 lemon
1 tsp lightly toasted pink
  peppercorns, coarsely
  ground
flaky sea salt
25g pecorino cheese, shaved,
  to serve

Shave the courgettes into long ribbons using a mandoline or speed peeler.

Put the ribbons in a large mixing bowl with the olive oil and lemon juice. Mix well, then spread out on a large platter so you can see the shape of the courgette strips. Finish with the pink peppercorns, a little flaky salt, and shaved or grated pecorino.

'Courgette caviar' is a Ukrainian spread made from slowly cooking summer vegetables down into a purée and it is delicious with so many things. You can have it on toast with soft cheese, stirred through pasta (as here), or use it to fill ravioli parcels. It keeps well and is a great way to handle a glut of summer tomatoes and courgettes.

courgette caviar and burrata rigatoni

SERVES **2**

150–200g rigatoni
2 small burrata
juice of ½ lemon
extra virgin olive oil, for
   drizzling
salt

FOR THE COURGETTE CAVIAR
(MAKES MORE THAN YOU NEED
FOR THIS RECIPE)

1kg courgettes (any colour)
50ml extra virgin olive oil,
   plus extra for storing
200g onions, thinly sliced
500g tomatoes (ripe and
   ready)
1 tbsp white wine vinegar
1 tbsp caster sugar

Use a mandoline to thinly slice the courgettes. You can halve them then cut them into half-moons or keep them in thin discs for more texture.

Put the oil and onions in a saucepan over a medium heat and cook for 10 minutes, or until soft and slightly browned. Add the courgettes and continue to cook over a medium heat for 20–30 minutes until they start to break down, stirring throughout.

Grate all the tomatoes on a box grater, leaving only the skin behind. Add the grated tomato to the mix and continue to cook for another 30 minutes, stirring frequently. Add a little water if things begin to brown too much, though a little colour here and there is a good thing.

Add the vinegar, sugar and a generous pinch of salt and cook for another couple of minutes just to take the edge off the vinegar. Remove from the heat and, once cooled, place in sterilised jars and top off with extra virgin olive oil before sealing with a lid. It will keep in a cool, dry place, but I like to keep mine in the fridge.

Cook the rigatoni in a large pot of seasoned boiling water till al dente, then drain and toss with a little olive oil and fresh lemon juice. Plate the pasta, put the whole burrata on top and finish with a generous quantity of courgette caviar. Mix it all up at the table, and you end up with a totally delicious creamy courgette pasta.

The courgette caviar will keep in the fridge in a sealed container for a few weeks.

Sometimes after school, my mom would take me for 'zucchini fries' at a place around the corner. It was a dark, smoky Hollywood spot with beat-up brown leather booths and those big red water cups, and I would eat the whole plate with two sides of ranch dressing. Looking back, she was probably just trying to get me to eat a vegetable, but it was a massive treat to me. Still is.

Over time, my homemade ranch dressing has become yoghurt based. If you use a good tangy yoghurt it's just as good as the original, in my opinion. The O.G. is usually made with mayonnaise and buttermilk and I can't be eating that much mayo on the regular.

courgette pané with yoghurt ranch

SERVES **4** AS A SIDE

2 or 3 courgettes, end
   trimmed off and halved
   widthways
125g plain flour
2 or 3 eggs, beaten
200g panko breadcrumbs
salt
neutral oil, for frying (I use
   rapeseed)
lemon wedges, to serve

FOR THE RANCH DRESSING

1 garlic clove, grated (use
   dried if raw is too strong
   for you)
grated zest and juice of
   1 lemon
1 tsp dried dill
1 tsp onion powder
1 tbsp cider vinegar (or
   preferred white vinegar)
pinch of salt
pinch of MSG
pinch of caster sugar
200g full-fat Greek yoghurt
   (or your preferred yoghurt)
handful each of chopped dill,
   parsley, mint and chives
splash of water

First, make the ranch dressing. Put the grated garlic, lemon zest and juice, dried drill, onion powder, cider vinegar, salt, MSG and sugar in a bowl, mix well and leave for 5 minutes. This mellows the garlic and hydrates the dried herbs/spices. Add the yoghurt, chopped herbs and water, mix well, taste and adjust for seasoning. Chill until ready to serve.

Cut each half courgette into 4–6 batons. Put them in a large colander and sprinkle with salt, making sure that each baton is seasoned. Mix well and leave at room temperature over a bowl (to collect the liquid) for 1 hour.

Set up your pané station. You can use three shallow trays or bowls: one with flour, one with beaten egg, and one with breadcrumbs. Discard the drained liquid from the courgettes and pat them dry with paper towels. Roll them in the flour, then the egg, and then the breadcrumbs, making sure they are evenly coated.

Heat enough oil in a deep frying pan or casserole to cover the courgette pieces until it reaches 175°C. You can shallow-fry them if you prefer – just make sure to flip them as they brown. Fry in small batches for about 5 minutes until golden brown and drain on a wire rack, seasoning them with a little salt while they are still hot.

Enjoy the courgettes with the ranch dressing and some extra lemon wedges for squeezing.

I had life-changing surgery as the result of an autoimmune disease when I was 32 years old. Stuck in bed for months before and afterwards, I was unable to eat properly for a very long time – torture for a greedy guts like me. Gloria, my then girlfriend's (now wife) housekeeper, is from Galicia in Spain and makes a delicious tortilla. It was a difficult time but Gloria's warm presence always made things a bit easier and the tortilla was one of the first things I remember enjoying again. Gloria often whips up tortillas for us, and I do my best to make them like hers. She wouldn't include anything other than classic potato, onion and egg but I like adding courgette – its mellow flavour adds a little summer glow. Just leave them out for a classic tortilla, adding one more potato instead.

a tortilla for gloria

SERVES **4**

2 courgettes, thinly sliced
1 large floury potato, peeled, halved and cut into 1cm-thick half-moon slices
1 white onion, thinly sliced
200ml olive oil
6 eggs
salt

Put the sliced courgettes in a bowl with a generous pinch of salt, give them a good mix and leave to sit at room temperature while you prepare the potato and onion.

Put the potato slices, onion, olive oil and a good pinch of salt in a medium frying pan, ideally the one you're going to make the tortilla in (I use a 20cm non-stick frying pan). It being filled to the brim really helps with the shape and final texture of the tortilla.

Put the pan over a medium heat and when the mixture just starts to bubble turn down the heat to low and cook for 20–30 minutes. If the onions start to brown too much, turn the heat down further – the onion should just slightly brown towards the end of cooking, the potatoes shouldn't brown. When they are done, the potatoes should be fork tender.

Squeeze out as much water as possible from the sliced courgettes and stir them into the potatoes and onion about a minute before the end of their cooking time, just for long enough to warm them through.

Break the eggs into a large bowl. Break the yolks with a fork and gently stir. Strain the oil from the pan into a bowl or jug (reserve this oil), add the warm potato, courgette and onion mixture into the eggs and gently fold together. Cover the bowl with a plate and leave for 5–10 minutes.

I rarely use non-stick pans, but it makes life a lot easier here.
continues overleaf...

a tortilla for gloria (continued)

Add a splash of the frying oil to the pan over a medium-low heat. Add the tortilla mix, giving it a gentle fold with a spatula or wooden spoon. If it starts to brown right away, the pan is too hot, and you'll need to turn down the heat. Cook for about 5 minutes (without stirring) or until you see that the edges are set and the mixture has a little less wobble.

Carefully flip the tortilla onto a plate that's a little bigger than the pan, then slide it back into the pan to cook the other side, quickly using your spatula to tuck in the edges. (Alternatively, you can slide the mix out onto a plate, put another plate on top of that and flip it over, then transfer it back into the pan – a bit less intense then flipping with a hot pan.) Cook for another 2–3 minutes or until it reaches your desired doneness: if you want it a bit runny in the middle, make sure the centre still feels soft to the touch – allow it to become firmer for something more solid. No matter what anyone tells you, it's good both ways and totally your choice.

Extra points if you use the frying oil to make a mayonnaise (see page 82) to go with it.

I'm a big Sun Ra fan, so when I discovered that he had a signature dish I dropped everything and learned how to make it. He would make Moon Stew for his 'arkestra' when they were short of money. When I make it, I imagine New York's east village in the Sixties, and what it would have been like to be in that house with the most supernatural musicians of all time, eating Moon Stew. There is no record of an exact recipe, so this is what I came to make with the information I could find. It's a very stripped-back recipe, with space for some variation (as long as it's made with love). I usually add a minced chilli, and some hot smoked paprika with the roux, and I like to have it with something to soak up the stew, like cornbread or crispy polenta.

moon stew and crispy polenta

SERVES 6–8

1 litre chicken or vegetable stock
1 tbsp vegetable oil
1 green chilli, finely chopped (optional)
4 garlic cloves, minced
1 tsp hot smoked paprika or chilli powder
1 tbsp plain flour
2 green peppers, deseeded and diced
2 white onions, diced
150g okra, cut into rough bite-sized pieces
6 plum tomatoes, quartered
2 sweetcorn cobs, quartered
salt and pepper
sincerity
love
Crispy Polenta (see page 233), to serve

Bring the stock to a simmer in a saucepan while you make a roux.

To make the roux, put the oil, chilli (if using), garlic and paprika or chilli powder in a large saucepan over a medium heat and cook, stirring, for 2–3 minutes. Add the flour and continue to stir until the mixture has the consistency of wet sand. Add a ladle of the warm stock and stir until smooth. Pour the roux into the broth while stirring, until evenly combined. Add the vegetables – along with some salt, pepper, sincerity and love – to the pan, then simmer for 30 minutes over a medium heat, depending on how soft you want the vegetables.

Serve with crispy polenta.

Play some Sun Ra, and get spaced out eating Moon Stew with friends and family.

Nasu dengaku – miso-glazed aubergine – is one of my favourite dishes, and I've adapted the Japanese recipe for courgettes. Achieving the perfect aubergine dish usually involves deep-frying, resulting in a confit-like texture inside, which is wonderful but too indulgent for me, at least for regular consumption. This technique for cooking courgettes yields a similarly tender texture without the need for deep frying. The miso glaze, traditionally made with mirin, sake and sugar, can be simplified using honey and miso for a delicious outcome. It's a great sharing dish, but we often have it in individual portions with steamed rice and carrot and ginger-dressed salad.

miso-glazed courgette

SERVES 2 AS A MAIN, 4 AS A SIDE

2 courgettes
neutral oil (I use rapeseed),
  for pan-frying
1 tbsp white miso paste (or
  to taste)
1 tbsp honey (or to taste)
white sesame seeds
squeeze of lemon juice
salt
spring onions, trimmed and
  chopped, to serve

Halve the courgettes lengthways and score each half in a crisscross pattern – you want the flavour to be able to get in there, so cut about halfway through. Season them with salt, rubbing it into the cuts thoroughly, then place them cut side down on a paper towel for 30 minutes – this will extract excess water, helping them tenderise without falling apart when cooked.

Dry the courgettes thoroughly and heat a few tablespoons of oil in a frying pan over a high heat. Add the courgettes to the pan cut side down and fry for 5–10 minutes, until golden, then flip and baste them with the oil for a few more minutes, so they cook through evenly. Transfer to a wire rack or paper towel to drain, then place the courgettes cut side up on a baking tray.

Preheat the oven to 200°C fan.

Whisk the miso paste, honey and a splash of water in a bowl until smooth and spreadable. Taste for seasoning, adjusting to your preference based on the saltiness of the miso, then spread a thin layer of the miso glaze over the cut side of the courgettes and sprinkle some sesame seeds on top. Bake for 7–10 minutes, ensuring the sesame seeds don't burn, until the glaze has caramelised.

Mix a little lemon juice into the remaining miso glaze. Spread it on a plate, place the courgettes on top, and garnish with chopped spring onions. Enjoy!

TOMATOES PEPPERS COURGETTES CUCUMBERS

When the process of breaking something creates unformed beauty, it is incredibly satisfying. If it also has a practical function, I'm sold. The jagged texture of the cucumber here creates more surface area to grab onto sauce and toppings. I learned the technique while making oi muchim, a Korean spicy cucumber salad, and have used it ever since. This version goes full Caesar and it's totally delicious.

smashed cucumber caesar

SERVES **4**

3 cucumbers, washed
3 tbsp panko breadcrumbs
1 tbsp extra virgin olive oil
2 garlic cloves, bashed (skin on)
4 thyme sprigs
grated zest of 1 lemon
handful of chives, thinly sliced
handful of parsley, finely chopped
salt and pepper

FOR THE DRESSING

4–6 tinned anchovy fillets in oil, crushed to a paste
25g Parmesan cheese, grated with microplane grater
1 egg yolk
15g Dijon mustard
juice of 1 lemon
1 tsp Worcestershire sauce
1 tsp Tabasco
100ml extra virgin olive oil

Smash the whole cucumbers using the flat side of a large knife until they start to break down, then roughly chop them into uneven, large bite-sized pieces. Put them in a colander over a bowl with a good pinch of salt, mix well and set aside for 15–20 minutes.

Meanwhile, toast the breadcrumbs in the olive oil in a frying pan with the garlic cloves and thyme till golden brown. Remove from the heat and season with salt and the lemon zest while hot, then set aside.

You can make the dressing in the same way as you would a mayonnaise, putting all the ingredients other than the oil into a bowl and mixing well, then slowly streaming in all the oil, whisking constantly throughout. Otherwise, blend all the ingredients at once in a blender (I often blend it). Check for seasoning.

Drain the cucumbers, then add them to the dressing with half the herbs. Mix well, then finish with the toasted breadcrumbs and the rest of the herbs.

I love Mexican ceviche in this style, but the shrimp can come and go without me caring. Heart of palm is my favourite thing to come out of a tin – I can easily eat a whole tin standing at my kitchen counter, and the texture and flavour are perfect for this dish.

Mexican ceviche is often made with Clamato (a tomato juice cocktail seasoned with salt, sugar, MSG, spices and clam juice), which is delicious in this, and in bloody marys and micheladas. Use it if you have it, but the grated tomato pulp, palm brine and seasonings here create a very similar experience.

heart of palm tostada

SERVES 4–6

4 tomatoes, halved
1 cucumber, finely chopped
1 red onion, finely chopped
2 red chillies or fresh
  jalapeños, finely chopped
bunch of coriander stalks,
  finely chopped
250g tin heart of palm,
  drained (reserving 1 tbsp
  brine)
Mexican hot sauce, to taste
juice of 4 limes
pinch of salt
pinch of MSG
pinch of caster sugar

TO SERVE

4–6 corn tortillas or tostadas
neutral oil, for frying (I use
  rapeseed)
2 tbsp mayonnaise
1 avocado, stoned and flesh
  thinly sliced

You can fry or bake the tortillas or tostadas until crispy: I prefer them fried. To fry, simply deep-fry them in a large pan of neutral oil heated to 180–190°C for 3–4 minutes until lightly golden, transfer to a wire rack, and season with salt while still hot.

Grate the tomatoes into a bowl using a box grater, leaving the skin behind, then add the cucumber, onion, chilli and coriander. Chop the heart of palm into pieces a bit larger than the cucumber and onion, then add to the tomato mix with the hot sauce, lime juice, palm brine and the salt, MSG and sugar. Leave to marinate in the fridge for 1 hour.

Add a thin layer of mayonnaise to a tostada, then some avocado slices, and finally a generous scoop of the 'ceviche'.

I highly recommend making a michelada drink to go with it. I always do!

cruciferous veg

The French have found many ways of making us feel special while eating a whole lot of butter, and when you spoon this sauce over a big beautiful golden head of cauliflower you too will feel special. Emulsifying sauces is like magic, a highly learnable magic that you won't soon forget.

whole roasted cauliflower with white miso beurre blanc

SERVES **4**

1 large cauliflower
2–3 tbsp extra virgin olive oil
salt

FOR THE BEURRE BLANC

100ml white wine vinegar
100ml dry white wine
1 tbsp white miso paste
1 large shallot, finely diced
200g cold unsalted butter,
  cubed

FOR THE VINAIGRETTE

1 part red wine vinegar
Dijon mustard, to taste (I use
  1 tsp per person)
3 parts extra virgin olive oil
pinch of caster sugar
salt and pepper

FOR THE SALAD

radicchio
fennel
parsley
dill

Preheat the oven to 180°C fan.

Being careful to keep the head intact, remove the core and trim the bottom of the cauliflower so it has a relatively flat surface – it should be able to rest upright. Generously coat the cauliflower in the olive oil and make sure all sides are seasoned with salt, rubbing it in to make sure as much is coated as possible. Place the head in a roasting tray, ovenproof pan or casserole dish, cover with foil or a lid and roast in the oven for 30 minutes. Remove the foil or lid and brush the cauliflower with a bit more olive oil, making sure it's evenly coated, and roast for another hour uncovered. It should be tender and golden brown all over.

Start making the beurre blanc about 20 minutes before the cauliflower is ready. Put the vinegar, white wine, miso and diced shallot in a saucepan over a medium heat. Let it simmer and reduce for 3–5 minutes, or until it's a glossy syrup. Strain the syrup into a bowl and discard the shallot, then transfer the strained syrup back into the pan and place over a low heat. Make sure your butter is very cold and in small cubes. Whisk the cold butter into the vinegar and wine mixture a cube at a time, ensuring each piece is emulsified before adding the next. *continued overleaf...*

whole roasted cauliflower *(continued)*

It will take a bit of time, but it will ensure a smooth sauce that shouldn't split. If the sauce splits, toss in an ice cube and whisk until it comes back together. Taste and check for seasoning, but the miso should have done the saltiness trick.

For the vinaigrette, simply combine the red wine vinegar and Dijon mustard in a bowl, then whisk in the oil gradually. Season with salt, pepper and sugar.

I think there is something so beautiful about the simplicity of spooning this perfectly toned sauce over the cauliflower and enjoying it with a side salad full of all the herbs you might otherwise be tempted to put over the top of it: handfuls of parsley and dill pulled apart and tossed with bitter leaves and the sharp vinaigrette.

I personally love coleslaw, but when people see it on a menu, they sometimes raise an eyebrow. If you're one of those people, no shade, I get it, it can be pretty gross. I'm not sure how people mess it up – it's basically mayo and vinegar – but it happens. This version has salad-cream energy with some hidden flavours that give it an edge.

white slaw

SERVES **4**

¼ onion, halved lengthways
  and thinly sliced
½ head white cabbage

FOR THE WHITE DRESSING

25g Dijon mustard
50g mayonnaise
50ml cider vinegar
30ml elderflower cordial
30ml extra virgin olive oil
salt and pepper

Soak the sliced onion in cold water for 5 minutes. Dry well with a clean cloth before adding to the cabbage.

Shave the cabbage paper-thin using a mandoline or sharp knife and put it in a large bowl with the onion and a pinch of salt, then mix and set aside.

Put all the dressing ingredients in a blender, with a pinch each of salt and pepper, and blend on high speed until smooth.

The cabbage will have released some water, so discard it before dressing with the white dressing. Add a little salt if needed, and some black pepper, before serving.

I grew up eating Nancy Silverton's recipe for chopped salad. My mother worked for Nancy and she often made it for us at home because we all loved it so much. This tinkered version came about as my wife doesn't always enjoy the cured meat in the O.G. recipe. We also almost always have tenderstem broccoli in our house. The smoky charred flavour goes perfectly with the tangy vinaigrette.

I've purposely not included salad quantities here, so you can make it your own.

charred broccoli chop salad

SERVES AS MANY YOU LIKE

tenderstem broccoli, stems
  halved
some garlic cloves, grated
lemon juice, to taste
iceberg or romaine lettuce,
  shredded
endive, shredded
drained tinned chickpeas
jarred pepperoncini peppers,
  thinly sliced
cherry tomatoes, halved or
  quartered
red onion, thinly sliced
provolone cheese, cut into
  batons
dried oregano, to taste
salt and pepper, to taste

FOR THE VINAIGRETTE

100ml red wine vinegar (or
  less if you want a less acidic
  vinaigrette)
juice of ½ lemon
½–1 garlic clove, grated on
  a microplane grater
1 tsp dried oregano
1 tsp Dijon mustard
1 tsp wholegrain mustard
100ml extra virgin olive oil,
  plus extra for drizzling
pinch of sugar

Lightly oil the broccoli, season it with salt and mix until evenly coated. Get a grill pan smoking-hot over a medium heat, then add the broccoli and cook for 5 minutes on one side. Transfer to a bowl and add some grated garlic and lemon juice while it's still hot, then mix and leave to sit at room temperature.

Chop lettuce and endive into roughly the same size pieces then place in a bowl and add drained chickpeas and the rest of the chopped ingredients. The only ingredient that requires a little extra attention is the red onion – run it under cold water for about a minute after slicing. This takes the edge off the heat and gives it a little extra crunch.

To make the vinaigrette, put the vinegar, lemon juice, garlic and oregano in a bowl and leave for a few minutes. This takes the edge off the garlic and hydrates the oregano. Add the mustards and gradually whisk in the extra virgin olive oil until combined. Season with salt and pepper, and the pinch of sugar.

Combine everything in a bowl, add a few spoons of the dressing and serve, drizzled with a little extra olive oil.

I've been serving this broccoli with jalapeño and almond sauce for years and it never lets me down. You take the whole stem and drag it through the bright 'pesto'-style sauce – it's a little spicy and super fragrant. I would deep-fry the broccoli until brown and tender, but this can be a bit sketchy for home cooking – the broccoli releases a ton of moisture, so it needs to be in a deep pan with plenty of space for the oil to bubble. The sauce is great with charred broccoli as well, so skip the deep-frying if you're not comfortable.

tenderstem broccoli with jalapeño and almond sauce

SERVES 3–4 AS A SIDE

200g tenderstem broccoli
1 tbsp extra virgin olive oil
lime juice, to taste
salt and pepper

FOR THE JALAPEÑO AND ALMOND SAUCE

6 spring onions, trimmed
2 fresh jalapeño chillies, deseeded if you want mellow heat
1 garlic clove, peeled but left whole
large handful of coriander (with stems)
1 thumb-sized piece of ginger, peeled
50g Parmesan cheese
50g whole almonds
100ml extra virgin olive oil
grated zest and juice of 2 limes

Char the spring onions, jalapeño chillies and garlic in a dry frying pan over a medium heat or under a hot grill, turning them so they char evenly. Remove the garlic when browned and the onions and chillies when burnt and blistered.

Put the charred vegetables and all the remaining sauce ingredients with a pinch each of salt and pepper in a blender or food processor and blend: you can keep going till it's smooth or leave some texture.

Dress the broccoli with the oil and season with salt and pepper before cooking on one side in a frying pan over a high heat for about 5 minutes. This gives the stems a deep char while keeping that fresh green flavour on one side. Remove from the pan and squeeze lime juice over them while the broccoli is still hot.

Spread the sauce over the surface of a platter and lay the hot, tender broccoli on top.

I have a hazy memory of an incredible warm salad I ate in New York for brunch one time - I recall it including sweet and savoury caramelised sprouts, crispy rice and a fried egg on top. I can't remember exactly where or when but it was a standout, so I've done my best to piece this together from memory. The combination of maple syrup, soy, and cumin is special, and I'm sure once you try it, you'll find ways to add it to other dishes.

crispy rice and brussels sprouts

SERVES 3-4

oil for frying (I use rapeseed)
200g jasmine/basmati rice (I use ready-cooked)
1 shallot (to make quick pickled rings)
20ml rice vinegar (or any vinegar you like to use)
pinch of sugar
10g cumin
30ml soy sauce
50g maple syrup
150-200g Brussels sprouts - trimmed, cut in half, and washed
200g mixed greens
1 handful mixed herbs - I like chives, parsley, coriander, and mint (but you can do you)
1 tbsp extra virgin olive oil
squeeze of lemon
eggs - 1 per person (optional)
salt and pepper to taste

The best way to make crispy rice is to boil it per the packet instructions - then spread it out on a tray and leave it in your fridge overnight. It dries the rice out, helping to keep the grains separate and absorb less oil when fried. I usually use the pre-cooked rice in a bag so I can get this together fast. The grains are a little undercooked and separate easily - I spread them over a tray and leave them uncovered in the freezer for 30 minutes while I prepare the rest of the ingredients. You can make a bigger batch of this crispy rice, as it keeps in an airtight container for 5 days.

Heat about 5cm of oil in a saucepan or Dutch oven/casserole - it should be about 175°C. Make sure you have at least 8cm of space between the oil and the top of the pan.

Remove the rice from the freezer and break it up into individual grains with your hands. It will be partly frozen and should come apart easily. Fry the rice in the oil in 2–3 batches for 2 minutes or until noticeably darker in colour. Use a fine mesh sieve to transfer it onto a paper towel and season with salt while still hot. Use the back of a spoon to break up any clusters while they are still hot.

Slice the shallot into rings (I used a mandolin), then put them into a bowl with a few spoons of vinegar, a generous pinch of sugar, and a little salt. Stir and set aside.

Put the cumin in a small saucepan over a medium heat, and when it starts to become fragrant, add the soy, remaining vinegar, and maple syrup. Allow it to bubble for about 2 minutes until it becomes a runny syrup consistency, then set aside.

You can roast or fry the sprouts – most of the time I've seen anything like this made in a restaurant they are fried – not only because it's delicious, but because it allows you to do it to order without leaving the sprouts to sit around, which is enemy number one of a sprout. The more time they chill the more time they have to get their stink on.

Fry them in oil at 175°C in small batches, for about 3 minutes. Transfer them to a bowl with a pinch of salt and some black pepper, then add the cumin glaze and give it a good mix.

If you are roasting them, add enough oil to coat the bottom of a baking tray, then place it in a 200°C fan oven for 5 minutes. Season the sprouts with salt before adding them to the hot oiled tray cut side down. Roast for 10 minutes, then flip and roast for an additional 10 minutes. Put them into a bowl with the glaze and give them a good mix.

Add the mixed greens, shallots, crispy rice, and herbs to the sprouts, then mix well. Add a little extra virgin olive oil and a squeeze of lemon before serving. If you're up for frying a quick egg, add that to the top.

People dream of California, especially LA where I'm from, and for good reason, as it can be a truly special place. However, when I was young, I dreamt of Europe. I was a skateboarder and spent most of my youth skating in parking lots and run-down schools or sitting in dense traffic jams. I could only imagine what it might be like to walk through a village with buildings older than the entire country I was from, eating food that had been prepared in a similar way for hundreds of years. I can hardly believe the journey I've made from those dreams to the life I have today.

On my first time in Puglia, I was in a small village, standing in the middle of a square anchored by a beautiful old church. It was better than I could have ever envisioned, and my first bite of food was orecchiette con le cime di rapa, little ears of pasta shaped by thumbs, served with bitter broccoli rabe, anchovy, a little chilli and crunchy breadcrumbs – it was perfect. This recipe is pretty traditional (I believe) other than the lemon zest in the breadcrumbs (I just can't seem to make breadcrumbs without adding some).

It can be hard to find rapini/broccoli rabe, so I often make this dish with tenderstem broccoli at home, ideally purple-sprouting as it's more bitter (broccoli rabe is in fact a type of turnip green, not broccoli as we know it).

continued overleaf…

broccoli pasta
with anchovy and breadcrumbs

SERVES **4**

300–400g dried orecchiette
400g tenderstem broccoli,
   trimmed (discard any woody
   stems) and washed
100ml extra virgin olive oil
2 garlic cloves, bashed and
   peeled
1 small fresh red chilli, bashed
   and left whole
6 tinned anchovy fillets in oil
salt
1 tsp dried red chilli flakes,
   to serve

FOR THE BREADCRUMB TOPPING

50g dried coarse
   breadcrumbs (homemade,
   using stale bread blitzed in
   a food processor, or shop-
   bought)
1 tbsp extra virgin olive oil,
   plus extra for drizzling
pinch of salt
grated zest of 1 lemon

Toast the breadcrumbs in the olive oil in a frying pan over a medium heat till golden brown, stirring constantly. Stir through the salt and lemon zest while the breadcrumbs are still warm and set aside.

Cook the pasta in a large pot of salted boiling water according to the packet instructions – when it's about 5 minutes from being cooked, add the trimmed broccoli.

Meanwhile, pour the oil into a large saucepan off the heat, add the whole bashed garlic, whole bashed chilli and the anchovy fillets. Place the pan over a medium heat and sauté for 3–4 minutes until the anchovies have dissolved into the oil. Add the pasta and broccoli straight from the water (allowing some of the water to come with them) and continue to sauté until everything is getting along nicely.

Remove the whole chilli and garlic and serve, topped with the breadcrumbs, chilli flakes, and some good extra virgin olive oil.

Good food should be a celebration of good ingredients, and this soup is a perfect example of that. I so often lean towards wanting big punchy flavours that play with sweet, sour and spicy but I am glad when dishes like this bring me back down to earth. This is the sort of meal that resets my palate and reminds me that great food can be very simple.

kale and white bean soup

SERVES **6**

500g dried cannellini beans
1 large carrot, peeled and left whole
1 white onion, peeled and halved
2 bay leaves
2 celery stalks
4 garlic cloves, 2 skin-on whole, 2 thinly sliced
4 thyme sprigs
3 tbsp extra virgin olive oil
100g trimmed kale or cavolo nero, roughly torn
100g Parmesan cheese, grated
salt and pepper
juice of 1 lemon, to serve

Soak the beans overnight in a bowl of cold water, then drain. Alternatively, put the dried beans in a saucepan of cold water and bring to the boil, then take off the heat and leave to cool before draining. These quick-soaked beans will have a similar texture, but overnight soaking is best.

Put the soaked and drained beans in a saucepan with the carrot, onion, bay leaves, celery stalks, 2 whole garlic cloves and the thyme. Add water to the pan until it sits about 5cm above the beans and bring to a rolling boil for 10 minutes, then reduce the heat and simmer for 15–20 minutes, adding a generous pinch of salt about halfway through. Remove the carrot, onion, bay leaves, celery, 2 garlic cloves and thyme when the beans are tender. Try three beans to test if they're ready, as often they can cook unevenly.

Put the olive oil and sliced garlic in a large sauté pan and cook over a high heat for 1–2 minutes until fragrant. Add the kale with a pinch of salt and sauté for 2 minutes, then transfer the kale, oil and garlic to the pan of beans. Stir through and check for seasoning, keeping in mind that you will be finishing it with Parmesan.

Serve with grated Parmesan, lemon juice, and a few cracks of black pepper.

Cauliflower purée makes a very welcoming bed, whether it's for a scallop, pork chop or grilled squash – it does its job, and well. It's a great lesson in how texture can transform the taste of an ingredient. When I learned how to make it, a technique was revealed to me that changed the way I look at food: you can cook a vegetable to the height of its flavour and blitz it into a creamy and savoury umami bomb, then all you need to do is pair it with a grilled protein or another vegetable, and you can basically cook.

cauliflower purée
with grilled squash or pumpkin

SERVES 4

1 Delica pumpkin or squash
extra virgin olive oil, for
  drizzling
3 banana shallots, roughly
  chopped
4 garlic cloves, roughly
  chopped
1 head cauliflower, broken
  into florets
3 tbsp cold butter
1 tbsp red wine vinegar
1 tbsp sweet white miso paste
juice of ½ lemon
salt and pepper

FOR THE GREMOLATA

5g mint leaves, finely
  chopped
15g parsley, finely chopped
grated zest of 2 lemons and
  juice of ½ lemon
30g toasted almonds, finely
  chopped
1 tsp ground cumin
4 tbsp extra virgin olive oil
1 tsp caster sugar
salt

Preheat the oven to 250°C fan.

Start by washing the pumpkin or squash – we are eating the skin – then cut it in half, remove the pulp and seeds, and cut the flesh into large pieces (big chunks produce a nice tender middle and crispy exterior without getting mushy). Coat the pieces in a generous quantity of olive oil, and some salt and pepper, and place on a baking tray. Roast for 20–30 minutes, until deeply browned on the outside and tender enough that a knife pushed through meets no resistance.

Meanwhile, put the shallots, garlic and cauliflower in a large saucepan with a tablespoon each of oil and butter and cook over a medium heat for 20–30 minutes, stirring often, until softened and lightly browned. Try to avoid letting them get fully caramelised – you want a cream-coloured sauce with a savoury flavour rather than a sweet brown purée. When soft enough to mash with the back of a spoon, transfer the mixture to a blender and add the vinegar, miso, the remaining 2 tablespoons of cold butter, lemon juice and some salt and pepper. Have a glass of water on hand as you blend, and add a splash if the sauce becomes too thick. Blend for 3–5 minutes. I know this seems like a long time, but the texture you get as a result is unreal.

To make the gremolata, combine the mint, parsley, lemon zest and juice, toasted almonds, cumin and olive oil in a bowl and season with the sugar and some salt.

Warm the purée in a saucepan over a low heat then spread a generous amount over the entire surface of your plate. Add the squash right out of the oven and spoon the zingy gremolata over the top.

I used to go to a deli in Santa Monica with my grandparents every couple of weeks. It was the kind of place that had desserts in a revolving display, and candy at the till. We would sit in the smoking section, and while my grandma chain-smoked Benson and Hedges, I would eat minestrone (because that's what my grandpa ordered). He would add Tabasco and crushed saltines, so I did the same. I can't remember a single other thing I ate there, but that soup stayed with me and this is my version of it. Adding the spicy pickled vegetables, Giardiniera (page 49), and brine reminds me of the Tabasco and adds a little texture.

hot and sour minestrone

SERVES **4–6**

150g ditalini or elbow pasta
4 bay leaves
1 sprig rosemary
2 sprigs thyme
50g unsmoked pancetta, diced
2 tbsp extra virgin olive oil, plus extra to serve
4 garlic cloves, whole and peeled
100g double-concentrated tomato purée
1 carrot, finely diced
1 onion, finely diced
1 leek, trimmed and finely diced
2 celery stalks, finely diced
400g tin peeled plum tomatoes
water or chicken (or vegetable) stock (enough to cover)
1 Parmesan rind, plus grated Parmesan to serve
400g tin cannellini beans, drained
1 small head cauliflower, broken into florets
200g Giardiniera (page 49), chopped, plus 1 tbsp brine
100g cavolo nero, tough stalks removed and leaves roughly chopped
salt and pepper

I usually cook the pasta separately and add it to the soup just before serving. This way I can store any leftover soup without soggy pasta. I also often cook more pasta than I need, so when the soup is done, I'll transfer whatever I'm going to eat to a new pan with some of the precooked pasta, and finish cooking it for a few minutes. Just make sure the pasta is cooked in salted water and is properly al dente (like undercooked) so it can finish in the soup and take on its flavour. If you're not planning on saving any pasta, just throw it in for the last 10 minutes of cooking.

Make a bouquet garni with the herbs by with wrapping kitchen string around them like a belt and tying it together. Set it aside.

Put the pancetta in a cold saucepan and place over a medium heat. When the pancetta has rendered its fat and is lightly browned, add the olive oil, garlic and tomato purée and fry, stirring continuously, until the garlic starts to take on a little colour. Add the carrot, onion, leek and celery and cook over a medium heat for about 10 minutes until the onion is translucent. Add the tinned tomatoes, water, Parmesan rind, bouquet garni and a good pinch of salt, bring to the boil, then reduce the heat and simmer for 15 minutes. Add the cannellini beans, cauliflower, chopped Giardiniera and cavolo nero, then simmer for another 10 minutes (adding the pasta now if you're planning to eat it all straight away). Add the Giardiniera pickling brine and some fresh cracked black pepper and stir through.

Serve with crusty bread, lots of good olive oil and grated Parmesan.

I convinced my mother-in-law to let me make this for Christmas Eve one year, along with baked potatoes and Swedish caviar, when she was living in Boston, USA. No one was really up for it and, to be honest, they all seemed a little annoyed with me. They loved it and ate their crow – we've had it every year since. It's a seriously comforting meal that we also have for dinner sometimes, with a poached egg.

cabbage and bacon

SERVES 4

3 tbsp extra virgin olive oil
6 smoked streaky bacon
  rashers, cut into 2.5cm
  pieces
1 white onion, cut into
  2–3cm-thick slices
2 garlic cloves, thinly sliced
1 head Savoy cabbage (any
  green cabbage will do),
  leaves separated and torn
  into large bite-size pieces
100ml chicken or vegetable
  stock, or water
2 tbsp white wine vinegar
2 tsp caster sugar
squeeze of lemon juice
salt and pepper

Put the oil, bacon, onion and garlic in a large saucepan or casserole dish over a medium-low heat. This is one of the rare occasions where one should not brown the bacon – cooking it slowly over a gentle heat helps the smoky flavour infuse through the entire dish without having to use much meat. After 10–15 minutes the onion should be starting to soften, and it should have a sweet smoky fragrance. Turn up the heat and add the torn cabbage leaves and the stock or water. When it starts to steam, cover with a lid and cook for 5 minutes.

Remove the lid and add a good pinch of salt along with the vinegar and sugar. Stir and cook for another 3–5 minutes. You can get a little colour on the cabbage here, but I prefer not to, in order to keep a sweet greenness to the dish.

Finish with a squeeze of lemon juice and freshly cracked black pepper.

I put this green slaw to work: it shows up a LOT at my table and never fails to make me look good. It's one of the easiest, big flavour, crunchy texture, punchy slaws you will ever make. It almost acts as a sauce, so it can bring the simplest meal together. I usually have it with grilled skin-on chicken or white fish like sea bass or bream. It's also great on the side of A Chickpea Stew for Francesca (see page 199).

green slaw

SERVES **2–3**

½ head white cabbage
salt

FOR THE GREEN SAUCE

3 spring onions, roots
** trimmed**
1 fresh jalapeño chilli (or any
** green chilli)**
50ml sushi rice vinegar
50ml neutral oil
thumb-sized piece of ginger,
** peeled**
25g coriander with stems
grated zest and juice of
** 2 limes**

Shave the cabbage into paper-thin slices using a mandoline or sharp knife, then put it in a large bowl with a pinch of salt, mix and set aside.

Heat a heavy pan – ideally cast-iron – over a high heat and when it's smoking hot add the spring onions and chilli and cook them for a couple of minutes until charred all over. You can do this under your oven grill if you prefer.

Remove the charred spring onions and chilli from the pan and leave to cool, then add to a blender with the rest of the ingredients for the sauce and blend until smooth. Check for seasoning and balance it out to your taste – if it's too sharp add some oil, and a bit more lime and salt if it's too sweet.

The cabbage will have released some water, so drain it before dressing it with the green sauce.

CRUCIFEROUS VEG

There are few things more satisfying than watching hot foaming butter being spooned over whatever needs it – in this case, you get to watch it fall through the layers of tender cabbage. It's methodic and theatrical but, most importantly, it makes things extremely tasty.

butter-basted cabbage

SERVES **2**

1 head sweetheart cabbage
100g salted butter
2 thyme sprigs
2 garlic cloves, bashed
  (skin on)
juice of 1 lemon
1 tsp Dijon mustard
splash of dry white wine
  (optional)
salt and pepper

Preheat the oven to 200°C fan.

Halve the cabbage lengthways (or quarter it if it's large), then put the pieces cut side down in a lightly oiled ovenproof frying pan over a medium-high heat and sear for 5–8 minutes until the cut sides are deeply golden (take it further if you like, if you want to get a charred flavour). Flip the halves so they are cut side up and transfer to the oven for 10–15 minutes until tender.

Remove from the oven and when the pan has cooled a little (if it's too hot the butter will brown too fast) add the butter, thyme and bashed garlic cloves over a medium heat. Tilt the pan so the butter pools around the aromatics, and when it starts to foam, begin basting the cabbage. It takes time for the butter to get through the layers of cabbage but just keep spooning it as it comes back. I usually baste for 2–3 minutes, a lot longer than you would with a steak as we're not concerned with overcooking.

Remove the cabbage from the pan and drain the butter back into the pan. Put the pan back over a medium heat and add the lemon juice, mustard, and a splash of water or white wine. Stir with a spoon until the sauce comes together. Put the cabbage back in and make sure that sauce gets everywhere.

Serve with a little black pepper.

CRUCIFEROUS VEG

Cooks love to painstakingly slice things and layer them to create the perfect texture – I'm pretty sure I've asked you to do this a handful of times in this book. Here, with this gratin, Mama Nature has already taken care of this for us, and this is a real celebration of those natural cabbage layers, with creamy sharp cheese sauce between each perfectly thin layer, sweet and delicious, topped with crispy breadcrumbs. I usually make this to eat as a main with a butter lettuce salad and a sharp mustardy dressing, but it also works as a side.

cabbage gratin

SERVES 3–4 (OR 4–6 AS A SIDE)

50g unsalted butter
2 garlic cloves, bashed (skin on)
2 thyme sprigs
100g panko breadcrumbs
grated zest of 1 lemon
2 sweetheart cabbages, halved lengthways
375ml whole milk
25g plain flour
1 tbsp Dijon mustard
100g Gruyère cheese, grated
100g mature Cheddar, grated
salt and pepper
lemon wedges, to serve

Put half the butter in a frying pan with the bashed garlic cloves and thyme and place over a medium heat. When it starts to foam add the breadcrumbs and toast, stirring constantly, till lightly golden. Remove from the heat, add a little salt and the lemon zest while they are still warm and set aside.

Steam the cabbage halves for 10 minutes and preheat the oven to 180°C fan.

Meanwhile, warm the milk in a saucepan over a low heat or in the microwave – it doesn't need to be really hot, just not cold. Put the remaining butter and the flour in a saucepan over a medium heat. Stir the flour into the butter as it melts, until it looks like wet sand, and cook for 3–4 minutes, then slowly add the warm milk, whisking until it's all combined, and the sauce is smooth. Add the mustard and cheeses and stir until melted. Season with a little salt and pepper.

Put the steamed cabbage halves on a baking tray cut side up, then spoon the cheese sauce between the layers before covering with an even layer of the breadcrumbs. Bake in the oven for 10–15 minutes or until golden brown.

Serve with lemon wedges.

This recipe is a bit of a two for one, as the cabbage tastes good with so many things and many different sauces would work with it. It is a useful side dish to know about. Equally, the romesco sauce happily accompanies most cooked vegetables and would be delicious served with grilled meat and roast potatoes.

tender cabbage with romesco

SERVES 2–3

1 head white cabbage, halved or quartered, depending on its size
1 tbsp olive oil
2 tbsp unsalted butter
½ tsp smoked paprika
2 garlic cloves, bruised whole in their skin
juice of ½ lemon
salt and pepper
Parmesan cheese, grated, to serve (optional)

FOR THE ROMESCO

4 tomatoes
6 garlic cloves (whole, skin on)
1 red pepper (or grilled pepper from a jar)
plenty of good-quality olive oil, for drizzling
thick slice stale white bread
1 red chilli, deseeded
25g unsalted almonds
25g unsalted hazelnuts
1 tbsp white wine vinegar
1–2 tsp hot smoked paprika

Start with the romesco. Coat the tomatoes, garlic, and red pepper (if using a fresh pepper) in olive oil, then blacken them under a hot grill for 20 minutes, turning them halfway through and removing the garlic after the first couple of minutes so it doesn't become bitter. Remove from the grill, place in a bowl, cover the bowl with cling film, and leave to steam for about 10 minutes before removing the blackened skin from the tomatoes and pepper with a paper towel, as well as the seeds and pith (don't run it under the tap, as this will remove most of the wonderful charred flavour). Set aside.

Fry the bread in a frying pan with a generous drizzle of the olive oil over a medium-high heat until golden brown on both sides. Set aside. Add the chilli to the same pan and fry over a medium heat for 2–3 minutes until fragrant. Add the nuts to the same pan to toast briefly before adding to a blender with the rest of the prepared ingredients (the tomatoes, garlic – with skin removed – cooked or jarred pepper, fried bread, toasted chilli, toasted nuts, 120ml olive oil, vinegar, paprika and some salt) and blend until combined. You can pass the sauce through a sieve to make it perfectly smooth, if you like.

Steam the cabbage pieces for 7 minutes, then put them in an ice bath to stop the cooking. Dry the cabbage on a tea towel and season with salt, making sure to get some in between the layers of leaves.

Heat the tablespoon of olive oil in a hot frying pan, then add the cabbage and fry on all both sides over medium-high heat for 5–10 minutes until deeply browned all over. Reduce the heat and add the butter, paprika and garlic. When the butter starts to foam, use a spoon to baste the cabbage with the butter, making sure it gets in between the layers. Finish with the lemon juice.

Warm the romesco gently then spread it over the base of a plate. Lay the cabbage on top of the romesco. You can finish it with some grated Parmesan cheese, but it's also perfect as is.

Something lovely that you'll find on menus throughout the Italian region of Puglia is broad bean purée and chicory. A classic yet humble Italian dish that's delicious and very comforting, it's typically served as a first course, but I'll often make it when I need something other than a potato next to my meat or fish. My wife is a big bean fan and will eat a vat of it on its own. I add lemon to the dish because I'm from California and I can't help myself, but other than that this is pretty 'traditional'. If you can get chicory, use it, but cavolo nero, kale, chard or spring greens will also do the trick.

broad beans and kale

SERVES **4**

200g dried whole broad
  beans or 400g tinned,
  drained broad beans
500ml chicken stock (if using
  tinned beans)
4 tbsp extra virgin olive oil
2 tsp dried chilli flakes
2–3 garlic cloves, thinly sliced
400g kale, cavolo nero,
  chard, spring greens or
  chicory, leaves torn
lemon juice, to taste
salt and pepper
bread (we often use
  sourdough as it is what we
  have on hand), toasted, to
  serve

FOR DRIED BEANS (OPTIONAL)

1 large carrot
1 white onion, peeled and
  halved or quartered
2 celery stalks
1 bay leaf
2 garlic cloves, smashed and
  peeled

If you are using dried beans, soak them in cold water overnight, then drain and put them into a saucepan with the carrot, onion, celery, bay leaf, garlic and enough water to cover. Bring to the boil, then reduce the heat and simmer for 10–20 minutes until tender, seasoning with a good pinch of salt halfway through. Drain and remove the vegetables, garlic and bay leaf, then blend using a stick blender or counter-top blender until creamy and smooth. Taste and check for seasoning and keep in a covered pan with a lid on until serving.

If you are using tinned beans, put the drained beans in a saucepan with the stock, bring to a simmer and cook for 5 minutes, then blend until smooth. Season with salt.

Put 3 tablespoons of olive oil in a large saucepan with the chilli flakes and garlic and place over a medium heat. Sauté for a few minutes, until fragrant, then add the greens (adding the hardiest leaves first) and cook for about 5 minutes. I like mine very tender, so I'll cook them for about 10 minutes, but 5 retains some brighter green flavour and more texture, if you prefer that. Turn off the heat and season with lemon juice, salt and pepper.

Make sure the broad bean pureé is warm before spooning it into a shallow bowl, then add the greens and finish with the rest of the olive oil and more lemon juice. Serve with toasted bread.

root veg

ROOT VEG

I was having lunch in a small village called Paradou in the South of France one summer when I first came across this dish. I saw it on the board and knew it was what I wanted, but I ended up ordering a very intense local dish made with fatty offal because, as a professional cook, I often feel this pressure to be an 'adventurous eater'. Luckily my wife ordered the vegetables, so I got to take small breaks from being brave to share what was her totally delicious meal. This dish encapsulates the concept of this book – perfectly cooked sweet and tender vegetables with a rich savoury sauce. Paradise.

spring vegetables with hollandaise

SERVES AS MANY AS YOU LIKE, BUT THE HOLLANDAISE IS ENOUGH FOR **2–3** PORTIONS

tinned artichoke hearts
new potatoes
asparagus
courgettes
broccoli
chives, thinly sliced
watercress
salt and pepper

FOR THE HOLLANDAISE

200g unsalted butter
2 egg yolks
juice of 1 lemon
pinch of cayenne pepper

First, clarify the butter for the hollandaise. I like to use a sealable plastic bag and simmering water, as it takes little effort and works perfectly every time, and you can make a large batch that's ready to use when needed. Put the butter in a sealable food bag, seal the bag, then place it in a pan of simmering water until the butter has completely melted. Transfer the bag to the fridge and leave until the butter has hardened – the liquid and whey will have separated from the now clarified butter. Separate the clarified butter from the liquid and whey and rinse it under a cold tap to clean it (it's solid, so the cold water will just wash off the rest of the whey).

When you're ready to make the sauce, gently warm the clarified butter in a pan until melted.

Put the egg yolks in a heatproof bowl with 1 tablespoon of water, then place the bowl over a pan of simmering water (making sure the bowl doesn't touch the water) and whisk them, moving them on and off the heat so they stay warm but don't scramble, for 2–3 minutes till they are light and thickened. *continues overleaf...*

spring vegetables with hollandaise *(continued)*

Add a squeeze of lemon juice, a generous pinch of salt, and the cayenne and continue to whisk over the pan of simmering water until combined, then slowly add the warm clarified butter, whisking continuously (like making mayonnaise) and adding a little more lemon juice or some water if it gets too thick, until it reaches your preferred consistency. Turn off the heat and leave the hollandaise bowl on top of the pan (giving it a stir every once in a while) while you prepare the vegetables. Otherwise, you can keep it in a Thermos until you need it.

You can steam, roast or blanch the vegetables. Here, I've blanched them.

All the vegetables can be cooked in the same large saucepan of boiling salted water. Start with the potatoes in cold water and bring to the boil, remove when tender and set aside.

You will need an ice bath for the rest of the veggies. I cook them separately until they are just shy of tender, then add them to an ice bath to stop the cooking and preserve their colour. Cook for 4–6 minutes, add to the ice bath until cooled, then transfer to a tea towel to dry.

When you're ready to serve, you can warm the vegetables by briefly putting everything back in the boiling water or microwave them for 30 seconds. Gently warm the artichokes through before serving as they should already be tender. Spoon a generous amount of hollandaise over the top and finish with chives, watercress and black pepper.

I love the French classic celeriac remoulade, and this is just an extension of that. The leek and apple help brighten things up and balance the rich, crispy goodness of the latkes, making a punchy combination of flavours and textures.

leek, celeriac and apple slaw with latkes

SERVES **4–6**

FOR THE LATKES

750g floury potatoes, peeled
250g white onions
20g dry breadcrumbs (I use
  panko as they are what
  I usually have to hand)
1 large egg, beaten
neutral oil (I use rapeseed),
  for frying
salt and pepper

FOR THE SLAW

1 leek
1 celeriac
1 green apple
1 tsp Dijon mustard
2 tbsp homemade or
  shop-bought mayo
2 tbsp white wine vinegar
juice of ½ lemon
1 tsp caster sugar

Grate the peeled potatoes and onions into a large bowl using the largest holes on a box grater. Add a generous pinch of salt, mix well, cover the bowl with a tea towel and leave for 10 minutes.

Place the mixture in the centre of a clean tea towel or muslin and wrap to make a bundle. Squeeze and squeeze over the sink until you've removed as much water as possible. This process may seem endless, but your hard work and patience will be rewarded with crispy, tender latkes.

Add the breadcrumbs, egg and a generous amount of black pepper to the mix, and make sure the egg and breadcrumbs are properly mixed in. You can taste a small piece of the raw mix for seasoning, although it may seem unappetising. Alternatively, fry a small bit to check if it needs a bit more salt.

Heat a 2cm depth of neutral oil in a frying pan over a medium heat, bringing the oil to temperature gradually to avoid it soaring past the ideal point and smoking excessively. *continued overleaf...*

leek, celeriac and apple slaw *(continued...)*

You can make your latkes large or small. I like to carefully place a heaped spoonful of mix in the oil and spread it out with the back of a spoon. Cook for 5–6 minutes until they are darkening at the edges and starting to pull away from the pan, then flip once and repeat before transferring them to a wire rack to cool. (Wire racks are preferable to paper towels for draining fried foods, as they allow cooked food to breathe on both sides, while paper towels tend to absorb oil but retain residual heat, resulting in soggy bottoms.) Season the latkes with a little salt while still hot.

Now, make the slaw. Trim the dark green tops from the leeks (keep them in the freezer for making stocks, soups, stew, etc.), then quarter the leeks lengthways. Now either separate some layers and cut them into long strips (julienne) or cut them widthways into thin crescents. Place in iced water while you prepare the celeriac and apple – this takes the edge off the leek and keeps it crisp. Peel the celeriac and cut it into thin disks, then matchsticks. You can cut the apple into matchsticks too, but I like thin half-moon slices. Leave the apples till just before you prepare the salad, so they are sweet, crispy, and don't discolour.

Add the Dijon mustard to the mayo in a bowl large enough to fit the slaw. Add the veggies, apple, vinegar, lemon juice, and sugar, and mix well. Pile the slaw on top of the latkes if you like the soggy-crunchy combo (it's how I do it) or on the side.

When my daughter Thomasina was three, she went through a phase familiar to many parents: she only wanted beige food. One day, her friend Felix was at our house play-cooking and told us, 'I am making green soup because it is Thomasina's favourite – she loves to eat green soup at nursery.' After some excited probing, we discovered this was true, and 'Green Soup' became a staple. The beauty is that it doesn't have to be the same every time – you can include kale, spinach or courgettes – but it is crucial to add frozen peas just before you blend, to make it a vibrant green as well as a little sweet. And then finally a chunk of Parmesan in the blender too to give it a salty, creamy edge.

green soup for thomasina

SERVES **4–6**

400g floury potatoes, peeled and cut into 4cm chunks
1 white onion, quartered
2 celery stalks, roughly chopped
750ml water
150g frozen spinach
handful of fresh spinach
250g frozen peas
2 tbsp unsalted butter
100g Parmesan cheese, roughly chopped
salt and pepper

Put the potato, onion, celery and water in a saucepan, bring to a rolling boil over a medium heat and cook for 10–12 minutes until the potatoes are falling apart, then reduce the heat to a simmer. Add the frozen spinach, and when it's thawed turn off the heat and add the fresh spinach and frozen peas. Put the mixture in a blender with the butter and chopped Parmesan cheese and blend until smooth, starting on a slow speed and slowly building up to high – keep on high speed for at least 1 minute. Taste and check for seasoning.

We always serve this soup with 'dippers': buttered toast cut into dippable pieces. And I'll often eat with her, adding some seasoned breadcrumbs (try the ones I make for the Cabbage Gratin on page 155, or the Broccoli Pasta ones on page 142), and some diced green chilli on top of my serving.

I'm personally not a huge fan of hot and hearty meals made with beetroot, like a risotto or a stew – the purple-pink colour throws me off for some reason. Yet I do love the flavour of borscht, and this recipe borrows a lot from it. Grilling the pickled beetroot is a nice way to add another dimension to its flavour and texture. When I have leftover roast beef, I'll add it to the salad, thinly sliced and cold from the fridge, as it mixes through wonderfully and you only need a small amount, though this is delicious and filling without it.

grilled pickled beetroot and horseradish salad

SERVES **4**

300g labneh or thick Greek yoghurt
thumb-sized piece of fresh horseradish (or to taste), grated on a microplane grater
3 tbsp creamed horseradish
handful of flaked almonds
6 baby pickled beetroots, halved
1 tbsp cider vinegar
2 tbsp extra virgin olive oil
handful of chives, thinly sliced
handful of parsley
handful of dill
salt and pepper

Mix the labneh or yoghurt, grated horseradish and creamed horseradish in a bowl, season with salt and pepper and set aside at room temperature (everything comes together quickly).

Lightly toast the flaked almonds in a dry frying pan over a low heat for a few minutes until golden, then remove from the heat and season with a little salt while they are hot. Set aside.

Get a griddle pan smoking hot over a high heat and add the beetroot halves cut side down with some weight on top – another pan or some grilling weights if you have them. Cook for 5–10 minutes, or until they have some dark char lines. I like them to get deeply charred (they can go a lot further then you think without tasting burnt). How quickly they char will depend on how much sugar is in the pickle brine, so keep an eye on them.

Take the pan off the heat, flip the beetroot and cover them so they can steam for a minute or two (this can be with another pan or a steel bowl, and it doesn't need to be a perfect fit). Slice the halves into uneven bite-sized pieces so the bright purple flesh is exposed on one side, then transfer to a bowl with the vinegar, olive oil and a pinch of salt – give it a good mix.

Spread the horseradish yoghurt over a large plate, then add the grilled beetroot, spooning the oil and vinegar over the top so it finds different spots to pool in the yoghurt. Add the chives, then add roughly torn whole leaves of parsley and dill fronds, and finish with the toasted almonds.

When in season, beetroots have a candy-like sweetness and an almost unnaturally vivid colour. They are abundant in the summer and available at most farmers' markets. Charring them intensely but briefly amplifies the sweetness while retaining a crisp texture. I often make this as a side to serve with grilled or fried meat or fish, but it does very well on its own. No matter what I serve it with, it gets all the attention, and I think it might be the most beautiful mix of colours one can put on a plate.

burnt beetroot salad

SERVES **3–4** AS A SIDE

2–4 beetroots (a mix of red, golden, candy stripe, or whatever is available at the market)
1–2 carrots (purple and yellow, or whatever is available at the market)
1–2 red chillies, thinly sliced
3 tbsp extra virgin olive oil
1–2 tbsp red wine vinegar (I prefer 2, but it's punchy)
200g feta, crumbled
handful of chives, thinly sliced
salt and pepper

Preheat your oven grill to high.

Wash and dry the beetroots and carrots, then lay them in a baking tray. Get the tray under the grill, as close as you can get, and grill until the skin is burned (use a barbecue grill if you like), then flip, so they have about 5 minutes on each side. You want to avoid cooking them too much; it's all about the char.

Transfer the beetroots and carrots to a large bowl of cold water and use a clean sponge or tea towel to scrub off the charred skin, without completely peeling it away (leaving a little char adds to the smoky flavour and cuts through the sweetness).

Use a mandoline to cut the whole vegetables into thin sheets, then mix in a bowl with the chillies, oil, vinegar, and a generous pinch each of salt and pepper. Mix well, then add the crumbled feta and sliced chives on top and serve.

Potato salad can cause problems for me, as I go full Gollum and can nail the whole thing in one go – high-class potato problems, I suppose. I think everyone should have a good potato salad on lock, as it's a blank starchy canvas that can show what you're all about. For me, it's creamy and briny with excessive amounts of herbs, capers, cornichons, olives and some sneaky fried shallots.

new potato salad with capers, olives and dill

SERVES **4–6**

1kg new potatoes, washed
2 banana shallots, halved lengthways then thinly sliced
neutral oil (I use rapeseed), for frying shallots (enough to cover)

FOR THE DRESSING

grated zest and juice of 2 lemons
100g mayonnaise
100g labneh or Greek yoghurt
75g capers, drained, plus 1 tbsp brine
100g cornichons, roughly chopped, plus 1 tbsp brine
150g spicy pitted large olives (I like Brindisa Perelló gordal olives picante), roughly chopped, plus 1 tbsp olive brine
big handful of parsley, roughly chopped
big handful of dill, roughly chopped, plus whole fronds
big handful of chives, thinly sliced
4 tbsp cider vinegar
salt and pepper

Put the potatoes in a large saucepan of cold water with a few generous pinches of salt (like pasta water) and bring to the boil. Once boiling, they should be fork tender after about 10 minutes. Drain and transfer to a large tray to cool at room temperature. If you want to peel them, just remove the skin while they are still warm – it will come right off.

Put the shallots in a cold saucepan and add just enough oil to cover. Cook over a medium heat for about 10 minutes until just lightly golden, then immediately transfer to a paper towel to drain (if you cook them for too long until they're deeply golden, they will probably be overcooked). Season with salt while they are hot, and set aside. Save the frying oil as we will use it for our dressing.

Mix 2 tablespoons of the shallot frying oil with the rest of the dressing ingredients in a large bowl, reserving the crispy shallots and some herbs for garnish. Season with salt and pepper.

Cut the potatoes in half or smush them with the palm of your hand and leave them whole. Mix it all together, checking for seasoning, and garnish with the remaining herbs and the crispy shallots.

I'm not sure you can think about beetroot as an ingredient without acknowledging its ability to turn things pink. It makes a very fun and delicious hypnotically pink dip, served with cold crunchy vegetables and hot bread. The American in me often gravitates towards the good qualities of ranch – it's sour and acidic while being creamy, with a little heat from raw garlic and fresh dill and chives bringing it all together.

pink ranch, cold vegetables and hot bread

MAKES PLENTY, FOR SHARING

1 cucumber, grated
250g whole pickled beetroot
  from deli counter or a jar
handful of dill
handful of parsley
bundle of chives, ½ finely
  diced
1 garlic clove, grated
grated zest and juice of
  1 lemon
1 tbsp cider vinegar
300g labneh
300g crème fraîche
3 tbsp extra virgin olive oil,
  plus extra to serve
salt and pepper

TO SERVE

carrots, cucumber,
  fennel, chicory, radishes,
  courgettes, or your choice
  of crudité
grilled flatbread (or bread
  of choice)
za'atar

Put the grated cucumber in a colander placed over a bowl, add a pinch of salt, toss and set aside.

Put the beetroot, half the herbs (leave the finely diced chives for stirring in after), the grated garlic, lemon juice, vinegar, and a good pinch of salt in a blender and blend until smooth. Transfer to a bowl and stir through the labneh and crème fraîche. Squeeze out the excess water from the cucumber and mix it into the dip, along with the olive oil, the remaining fresh herbs, and the lemon zest, saving a few leaves and a spoon of oil for the top. Taste and check for seasoning.

I love to put my cut vegetables onto a large platter on a layer of ice and serve it with flatbreads hot out of the oven, drizzled with a good glug of olive oil and sprinkled with za'atar.

I'm not sure there is anything more satisfying when cooking than layering paper-thin slices of potato with brown butter, pressing them overnight and frying them to create perfectly golden stacks of joy. Ideally, you would use a mandoline for this recipe, but you can grate the potato instead if you don't have one. I often serve these with salsa macha, crème fraîche and pickled kohlrabi, but the potatoes will be delicious with anything. They need to be prepared a day ahead, so I advise making a big batch and freezing the unfried slices, then you can fry or bake them from frozen another time.

confit potatoes
with salsa macha and pickled kohlrabi

SERVES 8–10 AS A STARTER OR FOR SHARING

1kg Maris Piper potatoes, peeled
125g unsalted butter
4 garlic cloves, crushed (skin on)
neutral oil, for frying (I use rapeseed)
crème fraîche, to serve
salt

FOR THE SALSA MACHA

100ml rapeseed oil
4 garlic cloves, roughly chopped
1 white onion, roughly chopped
1 cinnamon stick
1 star anise
15g dried chilli de arbol, deseeded and stems removed
15g dried chilli pastilla, deseeded and stems removed
60g unsalted peanuts
30g toasted white sesame seeds
1 tbsp rice vinegar

To prepare the confit potato, thinly slice the peeled potatoes with a mandoline or grate them coarsely with a box grater into a large bowl. Cover with cold water and set aside for at least 30 minutes.

Preheat the oven to 150°C fan and line the base and sides of a 900g (2lb) loaf tin with greaseproof paper.

Put the butter and crushed garlic in a saucepan and place over a medium heat. When the butter starts to foam and you can see it browning at the bottom of the pan, it's good to go. Remove the garlic.

Strain the potatoes, or squeeze out the water if they are grated, pat dry, then return to the bowl and add the browned butter (melted again if it's started to solidify) and a generous pinch of salt. Mix well, then layer the potatoes evenly in the lined tin. Press a layer of foil on top of the potatoes, then bake for 3 hours.

Remove from the oven, allow to cool, then transfer to the fridge with a weight on top and leave overnight. If you have another loaf tin, use it as a weight by filling it with water and putting it on top of the potatoes. Otherwise, you can use a bag of rice or beans.

To make the salsa macha, put the oil, garlic, onion, cinnamon and star anise in a saucepan over a medium-low heat and cook for 15 minutes, or until lightly golden. Remove the garlic and onion with a slotted spoon and discard the whole spices, retaining the oil in the pan.

**2 kohlrabi, peeled and
  thinly sliced (ideally on
  a mandoline)**
**3-2-1 pickling solution
  (see page 31)**
**dried hibiscus flowers
  (optional)**

Lightly fry the dried chillies in the same pan over a medium heat for 2–3 minutes until fragrant. Remove with a slotted spoon and set aside.   Fry the peanuts in the same pan for a couple of minutes until lightly browned, then remove with a fine-mesh sieve, reserving the oil.

Blitz the garlic, onion, chillies, peanuts and toasted sesame seeds in a food processor with 2 tablespoons of the frying oil (once it has cooled to room temperature), the vinegar and a generous pinch of salt until you have a coarse mixture, then combine it with the rest of the frying oil, mix and keep in a clean, sealed glass jar in the fridge (it will keep happily for a few weeks).

To make the pickled kohlrabi, put the kohlrabi discs in a large heatproof bowl. Heat your 3-2-1 pickling solution (see page 31) then pour it over the kohlrabi – if you want a pink colour, add a few dried hibiscus flowers. Alternatively, put the kohlrabi straight in the pan of heated pickling mix. Leave to cool at room temperature, then use straight away or store in the fridge where it will keep indefinitely.

Once the potatoes have been pressed overnight in the fridge, remove the foil and turn out the potato from the tin. Remove the greaseproof paper and cut into roughly 4 x 8cm rectangles (or any shape you like), then deep-fry in batches in a heavy-based saucepan of neutral oil heated to 160–180°C for 4–5 minutes until golden brown. Drain and season with salt while they are hot.

Serve a dollop of crème fraîche and the salsa macha with the potatoes, along with a serving of pickle.

When a vegetable can be sliced thinly like a sheet and layered, it absolutely should be – and often! Layers of flavour and texture create decadence while still being cosy and nourishing. This dish quickly went from a side to the main attraction in my home, often accompanied by a big butter-lettuce salad with quick-pickled shallots and mustard vinaigrette, and sometimes a fried egg.

root vegetable dauphinoise

SERVES **6**

500g Maris Piper (or other
   floury) potatoes, peeled
250g kohlrabi, peeled
250g celeriac, peeled
400ml whole milk
300ml double cream
2 garlic cloves, crushed
some freshly grated nutmeg
   (about 4 passes on a
   microplane grater)
softened butter, for greasing
salt and pepper
Gruyère, or any cheese
   you like, grated, to serve
   (optional)

Thinly slice the potatoes, kohlrabi and celeriac using a mandoline. Keep them in cold water until you're ready to start cooking.

Drain the vegetables and put them into a large saucepan with the milk, cream, crushed garlic, grated nutmeg, and some salt and pepper. Bring to the boil, then reduce the heat and simmer for 10 minutes.

Preheat the oven to 160°C fan.

Grease a large baking dish or casserole dish with softened butter (you can also rub a cut piece of garlic over the entire dish before buttering it – I like to). Add the vegetables in layers, adding the cooking cream as you layer. Pour the remaining cooking cream over the top, then bake in the oven for 30–40 minutes, or until a knife passes through the layers with little to no resistance.

It's good to go like this, or you can let it cool and cut it into nice rectangular pieces. Add a little extra cream and some grated cheese such as Gruyère or whatever cheese you fancy before reheating in the oven.

We have this with my cabbage and bacon dish (page 150) every Christmas Eve. It isn't a recipe as much as a way to make a basic potato feel special. I never use fancy caviar – I love it but only really eat it when someone else buys it for me. I discovered lumpfish roe while living in Sweden for a summer, and have never looked back. It's affordable, totally delicious, and a great way to make a simple meal feel super special.

baked potatoes and caviar

CHOOSE YOUR OWN ADVENTURE

baking potatoes

TOPPINGS

red lumpfish roe
black lumpfish roe
crème fraîche
butter
lemon wedges
loads of chives, thinly sliced
salt and pepper

I'm fussy when it comes to baked potatoes. I want the skin to be completely dried out and crispy, with an even, fluffy texture throughout. I wash them, making sure to give them a good scrub, then – while they are wet – I coat them with an even layer of sea salt or table salt and bake them on a wire rack in the oven at 200°C fan for 1 hour.

Timing is key – baked potatoes lose their sparkle pretty quickly. So I have all the toppings on the table ready to go: caviar jars in a bowl of ice, crème fraîche, butter, lemon, and the most chives you'll ever have to cut in one sitting.

The texture of this pearl-white soup is very smooth, and it's rich and comforting without feeling too heavy. I love it with a little smoked bacon but that can most definitely be left out – the paprika breadcrumbs also do the trick of adding smokiness.

celeriac and bacon soup with smoky breadcrumbs

SERVES **4**

25g unsalted butter
1 garlic clove, bashed and peeled
2 thyme sprigs
2 smoked streaky bacon rashers, cut into 2.5cm pieces
2 celeriac, peeled and cut into 2.5cm dice
1 large potato, peeled and cut into 2.5cm pieces
1 leek, white/light-green part only, cut into 2.5cm pieces and washed
750ml water or light chicken stock
1 tbsp white miso paste
salt and pepper

FOR THE SMOKY BREADCRUMBS

50g panko breadcrumbs
2 tbsp butter
1 tsp hot smoked paprika
generous pinch of salt

Put the butter, garlic, thyme and bacon in a large saucepan over a medium-low heat and sweat for 3–5 minutes, avoiding letting the ingredients brown. Add the celeriac, potato, leek, and water or stock, bring to the boil, then reduce the heat and simmer for 10–15 minutes until the vegetables are tender.

Put the breadcrumbs in a frying pan with the butter and toast over a medium heat for a few minutes until golden brown, stirring constantly, then remove from the heat and add the paprika and salt while they are still warm.

Remove the thyme sprigs and put the soup into a blender with the miso and a few twists of fresh cracked pepper, then blend until smooth for a good minute or two – blending it for this long makes a noticeable difference to the texture. Check for seasoning – it will probably need some salt, depending on the saltiness of your miso and bacon. I like to pass it through a sieve to make sure it's extra smooth but it's not a deal breaker.

Serve with the smoky breadcrumbs on the side for sprinkling – I like to add them as I eat, so they keep their crunch.

I hadn't been in a professional kitchen for almost a decade when, on starting at Orasay in London, the first job I was given was peeling roasted beetroot. The chef would bury the beetroot in hot coals at the end of service and they would be prepped the next day. They become incredibly tender and the colour bleeds all over whatever you put them with in the most beautiful way – I was so happy to be back in the kitchen watching the magic happen. This recipe gets close to this with roasting and oven-grilling, but try burying them in the coals at your next barbecue – it's delicious and totally satisfying.

roasted beetroot and baba ganoush

SERVES **4**

6 medium to large beetroot, scrubbed clean in cold water
4 tbsp extra virgin olive oil, plus extra for drizzling
1 tbsp red wine vinegar
handful of dill, roughly chopped
handful of parsley, roughly chopped
handful of mint, roughly chopped
salt and pepper
warm flatbread, to serve

FOR THE BABA GANOUSH

2–3 aubergines
1 garlic clove, grated
juice of 1 large lemon
60g tahini
3 tbsp extra virgin olive oil
1 tsp cumin seeds
1 tsp dried chilli flakes

Preheat the oven to 220°C fan.

Wrap the scrubbed beetroot in a large sheet of foil, adding the olive oil and a pinch of salt, and enclose to form a parcel. Put them in a baking paper-lined baking tray and roast in the oven for 1 hour.

Remove the foil and put the beetroots back on the tray and under a hot grill as close as you can get them for 10 minutes, flipping them halfway through.

Leave the beetroots to cool until you can handle them – the hotter they are the easier it will be to remove the skin. I wear gloves and work off as much of the skin as possible by rubbing it by hand, only using a small knife to trim any skin or char that's left behind. Set the beetroots aside.

To make the baba ganoush, first cook the aubergines. Start by piercing a few shallow holes in the aubergines with the tip of a knife, then cook over an open flame, rotating the aubergines every 3–4 minutes, or under a hot oven grill for 20 minutes, flipping them halfway through. They should be completely charred on all sides and the inside should be soft. Transfer to a bowl, cover tightly with a lid or cling film and leave to steam and cool for 5 minutes. Remove the burnt skin from the aubergines: I like to use a paper towel to wipe away all the smaller pieces of char.

While the aubergines cool, put the grated garlic, lemon juice and a pinch of salt in a mixing bowl, mix and set aside. This takes the edge off the raw garlic. Roughly chop the aubergine flesh, then add it to the lemon and garlic along with the tahini and some black pepper. Mix with a fork or whisk until combined. Adjust the salt and lemon to taste.

Cut the beetroots into large uneven pieces about the size of two bites. You can have these at room temperature or quickly flash them in a hot oven before seasoning. I love them hot over the room-temperature baba ganoush. Season with salt and pepper, and the red wine vinegar, dill, parsley and mint.

Put the olive oil, cumin seeds and chilli flakes in a frying pan over a medium heat and when the oil starts to spit, turn off the heat and season with salt. Spoon over the baba ganoush while it's hot, just before serving.

Spoon the warm beetroot over the baba ganoush with lots of olive oil. Serve with warm flatbread.

This recipe is very close to a standard dal, with the carrots adding some sweetness and a focus on the flavour of cumin both in the base and the fragrant ghee topping. It's a comforting meal and often shows up in the middle of the week in my household. The ghee topping really adds something special to this kind of dish, and it's a great way to finish lots of curries.

carrot and cumin dal
with crispy chickpeas and spiced ghee

SERVES **4–6**

2 tbsp neutral oil (I use rapeseed)
2 red onions, finely diced
1 tomato, diced
1 thumb-sized piece of ginger, grated
2 or 3 carrots, peeled and diced
2 garlic cloves, minced
1 tbsp ground cumin
1 tsp ground turmeric
1 tsp ground coriander
200g red lentils, rinsed and drained
1 litre water
juice of ½ lemon
1 tsp garam masala
fresh coriander, to serve

FOR THE CRISPY CHICKPEAS

400g tin chickpeas, drained and patted dry with paper towel
1 tbsp neutral oil (I use rapeseed)
generous pinch of salt

FOR THE GHEE TOPPING

2 tbsp ghee
1 tbsp cumin seeds
1 tsp dried red chilli flakes
1 tsp chilli powder

Heat the oil in a saucepan over a medium heat, add the onions, tomato, ginger and carrots and sweat for 5–10 minutes until they start to soften and slightly brown, then add the garlic and all the dried spices except the garam masala (you'll add that at the end) and cook for a few minutes. Add the rinsed, drained lentils and stir to make sure everything is mixed before adding the water. Bring to the boil, then reduce the heat and simmer for 30–40 minutes or until the lentils start to break down.

Preheat the oven to 200°C fan.

While the dal is cooking, coat the drained and dried chickpeas with the oil on a baking tray and roast for about 20 minutes, shaking them halfway through, until golden brown. Season with the salt as soon as you remove the tray from the oven.

When the lentils are cooked, turn off the heat and add a generous pinch of salt with the lemon juice and garam masala. If you like, you can use a stick blender to blend a cup of the dal and put it back in for a smoother finish.

Put the ghee and a couple of cumin seeds in a small frying pan and place over a medium heat. When the cumin seeds begin to pop, add the rest of the cumin seeds, along with the dried chilli flakes and chilli powder and stir for about 30 seconds before spooning the hot, fragrant ghee over the dal. Add some torn fresh coriander and enjoy.

This was one of the most successful recipes I ever shared online, and people regularly send me photos of themselves making it, which I love to see. If you don't want to use the bacon, it can easily be left out. You can leave the butter bean mix whole or blend it into a smooth sauce. I love it blended here, as it feels super rich and indulgent even though it's just a bunch of beans. Cooking the carrots in two stages creates a seriously tender texture and gets you there relatively quickly.

carrots and butter beans

SERVES **2**

4–6 carrots, peeled
2 tbsp olive oil
4 thyme sprigs
1 large white onion, thinly
  sliced
50g smoked bacon, roughly
  chopped, or lardons
4 garlic cloves, thinly sliced
400g tin butter beans, with
  liquid
120ml white wine, chicken or
  vegetable stock, or water
juice of ½ lemon
1 tbsp cider vinegar
salt

FOR THE TOPPING

2 tbsp flaked almonds
1 fresh jalapeño chilli (or your
  favourite green chilli), finely
  chopped
handful of parsley, finely
  chopped
squeeze of lemon juice
1–2 tbsp olive oil
pinch of salt
pinch of sugar

Steam the carrots for 7–10 minutes until they've softened but still have some bite, then transfer to a bowl of cold salted water. Cut each carrot lengthways, pat dry with kitchen paper, then fry in a frying pan over a high heat with a tablespoon of olive oil, ideally pressing them with a weight as they cook (use a heavy pan) and turning them once, until nicely golden and seared.

To make the bean purée, put the thyme, onion, bacon and garlic in a small frying pan with a tablespoon of olive oil and sauté over a medium heat for about 10 minutes until soft and lightly browned, then add the beans, wine, stock or water and simmer for about 5 minutes. Transfer to a blender along with the lemon juice and vinegar and blend for 2 minutes at medium speed, then an extra 2 minutes on high speed. Add a splash of water to loosen the mixture if needed. Season with salt to taste.

To make the topping, toast the almonds and chilli in the same pan that you cooked the carrots in over a medium heat for about a minute. Transfer to a bowl and add the parsley, lemon juice, olive oil, and the salt and sugar.

Warm the purée if necessary, spoon it onto serving plates, then top with the carrots and finish with the green topping.

beans

peas

corn

pulses

If you've ever wanted to make a showy spectacle out of some green beans - I got you. This is one for the barbecue, so save it for a day when you plan on lighting it up. It's a beautiful presentation, but also gives a great mix of texture and flavour - some beans are deeply charred, while others are only steamed with a light smoky flavour. You will need food-grade butchers' twine that's been soaked in water for a few minutes before use. The sauce is Pierre Gagnaire's L'express sauce - a simple sauce made of high-quality ingredients that I can't get enough of, especially with vegetables.

trussed green beans

SERVES **4–6** AS A SIDE OR
2–3 AS A MAIN

400g green beans (200g per
   bundle)
130g double concentrated
   tomato purée
30g Dijon mustard
200ml white wine
1 tsp cayenne pepper,
   optional
100ml double cream
2 tbsp extra virgin olive oil
1 lemon
salt and pepper to taste

Soak a generous length of butcher's twine in water for 2-3 minutes.

Put the tomato purée, mustard, and white wine into a saucepan over a medium heat. Cook for 10 minutes stirring throughout - the sauce will bubble and spit unattended so keep stirring. When the wine has almost completely reduced, and you have a thick sauce, add the cayenne pepper and cream, then continue to cook until you have a custard-like consistency - about 2-3 minutes. Season with salt and pepper.

Season the beans with extra virgin olive oil, salt, and pepper. Mix well, then wrap with the soaked twine, with 2-3 ties depending on the length of the beans. Grill, avoiding too much contact with the open flame, until charred all over. Squeeze fresh lemon and some olive oil over the finished beans.

I like to plate the beans still wrapped, in a bed of the sauce.

Whenever we ordered Chinese takeout as a kid, I made sure sesame noodles were in the mix – cold and covered in a peanut and sesame sauce. It was what I usually hoovered up first. This particular riff is made with green beans and smashed cucumber and is full of flavour. You can include noodles, of course, to bulk it up, and it would be great with some crispy chickpeas or a poached egg too.

cold, spicy sesame and peanut green beans

SERVES **2**

200g green beans
150g cucumber
10g fresh coriander, roughly chopped
1 tbsp toasted sesame seeds
your favourite chilli oil, to taste

FOR THE SPICY SESAME AND PEANUT SAUCE

50g peanut butter (chunky or smooth)
50g toasted sesame paste or tahini
1 tbsp Chinese black vinegar
1 tsp light soy sauce
15g honey
1 garlic clove, grated on a microplane grater
thumb-sized piece of ginger, peeled and grated on a microplane grater
2–3 tbsp hot water

Blanch the green beans in salted boiling water for 3 minutes, then transfer to a salted ice bath to cool. I always season my ice bath with some salt for vegetables if there isn't another stage of cooking to come – it helps retain their flavour and stops them tasting too watery. Remove the beans from the bath once they are cool and leave on a clean, dry towel to drain any excess water.

Using the side of a knife, smash the cucumber until it is just about all coming apart. The smashing creates more surface area for the sauce to cling onto. Season with salt and leave it to sit in a bowl while you make the sauce.

Put all the sauce ingredients in a bowl and mix until combined, adding the hot water in stages (the sesame and peanut butter seize up, so this helps loosen it). The sauce should just be able to run off your spoon. Check for seasoning and add a pinch of salt and a bit more honey if needed.

Bring everything together in a bowl.

Cooking for my wife and children brings me a lot of joy, but I'm conscious that my wife, Francesca, doesn't want to subsist on the type of full-on teenager diet that I can end up on if I'm unchecked, and we certainly don't want the kids to either. Family meals keep me off that track and I've finally honed how to hit that delicious yet nutritious combo. I remember the first time my wife asked me to make a 'chickpea stew-type thing' for dinner. It wasn't something I had on lock, so this marked the start of a journey. Initially, it was something that I made just for her, but it has evolved into something I make for all of us. It's cosy and filling, but also makes me feel like I'm going to live forever when I eat it.

a chickpea stew for francesca

SERVES 3–4

2 tbsp neutral oil (I use rapeseed)
2 garlic cloves, finely chopped
thumb-sized piece of ginger, peeled and grated on a microplane grater
1 red chilli, deseeded and finely diced
1 onion, chopped
250g fresh tomatoes (whatever you have to hand), roughly chopped
100g double-concentrate tomato purée
400g tin full-fat coconut milk
400g tin peeled plum or chopped tomatoes
1 courgette, diced
400g tin chickpeas, drained, plus 1 tbsp tin liquid
1 tbsp cider vinegar
2 tsp sugar or honey

FOR THE SEASONED YOGHURT

½ cucumber
225g Greek yoghurt or plain yoghurt
grated zest and juice of 1 lemon
handful of herbs (parsley, coriander or mint), roughly chopped

Grate the cucumber for the seasoned yoghurt into a bowl using a box grater and season it with a good pinch of salt. Mix well and set aside at room temperature.

Put the oil, garlic, ginger, chilli, onion and half the fresh tomatoes in a large saucepan or casserole dish over a medium heat and cook for about 10 minutes, until softened and fragrant. Season with a generous pinch of salt, then add the tomato purée and cook for 5 minutes, stirring often. Add the coconut milk and tinned tomatoes – crushing the tomatoes with your hands as you add them if using plum tomatoes – and bring to the boil, then reduce the heat and simmer for 5 minutes. Add the courgette, chickpeas and the remaining fresh tomatoes, then simmer for another 5–10 minutes. Finish with the chickpea water, vinegar and the sugar or the honey.

Drain and squeeze the excess moisture out of the grated cucumber. Mix it with the yoghurt, lemon juice and zest and the herbs and season with salt and pepper.

Put a few scoops of the seasoned yoghurt on top of the stew before serving. Leave it on top, scooping a bit with each bite as opposed to mixing it through.

Sadly, I didn't have fried plantains, or any proper Caribbean food, until I moved to London in 2006. I mourn for all those years without it in my life. The last few bites of a dish, when you mop up the last of your gravy with plantain, is always a highlight, and this is a meal made of that moment.

fried plantain and jerk beans

SERVES 3–4

50g smoked bacon lardons
1 white onion, thinly sliced
4 thyme sprigs
neutral oil, for frying (I use rapeseed)
½ head savoy cabbage, core removed, leaves roughly chopped
400g tin kidney beans, drained
400g tin black beans, drained
250ml chicken or vegetable stock, or water
2 ripe plantains, peeled and sliced thickly at an angle
salt and pepper

FOR THE CORIANDER SAUCE

handful of coriander (leaves and stems)
100g mayonnaise
15g pickled ginger (see page 31 or use shop-bought), plus 20ml pickled ginger vinegar
salt

FOR THE JERK SEASONING

2 tbsp light soy sauce
2 tbsp Worcestershire sauce
1 tbsp cider vinegar
50g double-concentrated tomato purée
6 garlic cloves, peeled and left whole
1 scotch bonnet chilli (I remove the seeds, otherwise no one will eat it with me)
1 large thumb-sized piece of ginger, peeled
30g dark brown sugar
1 tsp ground cinnamon
½ tsp ground cloves
1 tsp dried thyme
2 tbsp water

Put the lardons, onion, thyme sprigs and a tablespoon of oil in a large saucepan or casserole dish over a medium heat and cook, stirring occasionally, for 10 minutes, until softened and lightly browned.

Blend all the ingredients for the coriander sauce in a blender until smooth. Transfer to a bowl and set aside.

Rinse out the blender, then add all the jerk seasoning ingredients and blend until smooth. Add the jerk mix to the pan of lardons and onion with a pinch of salt and some black pepper and cook over a medium heat, stirring often, for 15–20 minutes until it reduces and thickens. Add the cabbage, drained beans and stock and simmer for 5 minutes. The sauce should be glossy and not too thick. Remove from the heat and set aside while you fry the plantains, removing and discarding the thyme sprigs.

Heat a 2cm depth of neutral oil in a high-sided frying pan over a medium heat, then add the plantains and fry in batches for 6–8 minutes until golden brown all over. Season with salt while they are still hot.

Serve the beans on a plate, with the plantains and coriander sauce on another.

Getting some fire under peas adds a subtle smoky flavour and tightens their skin, giving them a little extra pop when you bite into them. If you don't have a gas hob, you can try grilling them at your next barbecue or cooking them in a smoking-hot cast-iron pan with no fat. This method tastes more charred than smoky but it is delicious nonetheless.

grilled peas, pickled tomato and burrata

SERVES 3–4

6–8 pickled tomatoes (see page 31 for 3-2-1 method and use peppercorns), plus a splash of the pickling liquid
200g frozen garden peas
3 tbsp extra virgin olive oil
½ green chilli, diced
6–8 chives, thinly sliced
handful of basil leaves, thinly sliced
handful of mint leaves
250g burrata
salt

FOR THE SEASONED BREADCRUMBS

50g panko breadcrumbs
extra virgin olive oil
pared peel of ½ lemon
1 garlic clove, smashed (skin on)
1 sprig of rosemary or thyme

First, pickle the tomatoes following the method on page 31 and toast the breadcrumbs. You need to do this a little ahead (about 30 minutes).

To toast the breadcrumbs, heat a generous amount of olive oil in a frying pan over a medium heat along with the lemon peel, smashed garlic and rosemary or thyme. Add the breadcrumbs and toast for a few minutes till golden brown, then season with salt.

Grill the peas from frozen in a fine-mesh sieve over an open flame. Try to avoid getting the mesh too hot and keep them moving – they will be ready in 3–4 minutes.

Put the peas into a bowl with a pinch of salt and the olive oil, chilli, chives, basil and mint. Add the pickled tomatoes and a splash of their pickling liquid just before serving (if you let the peas sit in the vinegar for too long, it will start to dull their vibrant colour). Mix well and spoon over some broken burrata, adding 2–3 tablespoons of the toasted breadcrumbs at the very last second, so they stay crunchy.

Growing up in LA, you were never too far from someone selling elotes, or 'Mexican street corn'. Near my home in west LA it was sold from small carts: when ordered, the corn was pulled out of the steamer and slathered with a mixture of mayonnaise and Mexican crema (a tangy sauce similar to sour cream), then topped with crumbly cotija cheese (feta is its closest equivalent outside Mexico), chilli powder and lime juice. Succotash – a combination of sweetcorn and broad beans with chilli and herbs – is, on the other hand, usually a relatively bland side dish that pops up around Thanksgiving, but when these two dishes merge it's a beautiful thing. I often add smoked lardons to the mix (with the onion), when making this for meat-eaters. A poached egg on top is always welcome.

elote succotash

SERVES **4–6**

100g podded broad beans
  (peeled, if needed)
6 sweetcorn cobs
1 tbsp unsalted butter
1 white onion, finely diced
1 green pepper, deseeded
  and finely diced
2 garlic cloves, grated or
  finely chopped
1 fresh jalapeño or red chilli,
  finely diced
25g crème fraîche
25g mayonnaise
juice of 2 limes
1 tbsp white wine vinegar
1 tsp caster sugar
1 tsp chilli powder
200g feta cheese
10g chives, finely chopped
10g coriander (including
  stems), finely chopped
salt

If the broad bean skins are tough, blanch the beans in boiling water for 1 minute then transfer them to a bowl of iced water, drain and peel. You can eat them skin on if you prefer.

Stand the corn cobs upright on a chopping board and run a sharp knife around the cobs to remove the kernels. Cut the kernels from the cob, then cook in salted boiling water for 5 minutes. Drain and set aside.

Put the butter, onion, pepper, garlic, chilli and a pinch of salt in a large saucepan, place over a medium heat and cook for about 10 minutes until softened (add the broad beans with the onion if you're keeping the skin on). Add the cooked corn (and the peeled broad beans, if skin has been removed) along with another pinch of salt, then cook for another 2–3 minutes, so the corn is warm but still has texture. Add the crème fraîche and mayonnaise and warm through for about a minute, then turn off the heat and add half the lime juice along with the vinegar, sugar, chilli powder, half the feta (crumbled), and most of the herbs, reserving some for garnish. Mix well and serve with the rest of the lime juice, and the rest of the feta and herbs on top.

This might seem like a basic dish, but the process of making it is a great example of how you layer the flavour of a whole vegetable to get the most out of it, using the cobs to make broth, blending the kernels to create a creamy texture, and adding barley-cooked kernels for a sweet crunch. I love to have this with blackened fish, grilled shrimp or fried chicken.

cream corn

SERVES 4–6 AS A SIDE

4–6 sweetcorn cobs
2 tbsp unsalted butter
25g smoked bacon lardons
1 white onion, finely chopped
2 garlic cloves, finely
  chopped
2 fresh jalapeño chillies
200g tin sweetcorn in brine
50g crème fraîche
salt and pepper

Cut the kernels from the fresh cobs into a bowl, standing them upright on a chopping board and running a sharp knife around the cob to remove the kernels. Put the cobs into a saucepan with just enough water to cover and bring to the boil, then reduce the heat and simmer. After about 20 minutes, when the water has reduced by half, turn off the heat and set aside, leaving the cobs to steep.

Put 1 tablespoon of the butter in a large saucepan along with the lardons, onion, garlic and 1 jalapeño and sauté over a medium heat for 10 minutes. Add the tinned sweetcorn and brine and continue to cook for 5 minutes, then add the corn broth. Bring to the boil, then reduce the heat and simmer till it's almost completely reduced. Put the mixture into a blender with a pinch each of salt and pepper, and the remaining tablespoon of butter, and blend until smooth.

If corn is in season, I mix the kernels through raw. If not, I blanch them in boiling salted water for 3 minutes before draining and stirring them through the blended mixture with the crème fraîche. Check the seasoning and finish with diced jalapeño on top or mixed through.

onions

leeks

aubergines

mushrooms

Cheese and onion is a flavour combination that many people come to love as kids. This dish is a celebration of that popular combo in a 'grown-up' package. Savoury cheese mixed through creamy beans topped with sweet and tender onions. It's a simple, beautiful meal that I often enjoy with fennel slaw, some nice bread and a little green chilli and parsley oil.

roasted shallots, chorizo and creamy beans

SERVES **4**

8–10 banana shallots, peeled
6 tbsp extra virgin olive oil
120g dried, cured Spanish
  chorizo, diced
2 thyme sprigs
grated zest and juice of
  1 lemon
1 tsp fennel seeds
2 garlic cloves, thinly sliced
2 x 400g tins cannellini beans,
  plus all the liquid from the
  tins
230ml chicken or vegetable
  stock
120ml dry white wine
50g pecorino cheese, grated
handful of parsley, roughly
  chopped
salt and pepper

Preheat the oven to 180°C fan.

Halve the peeled shallots lengthways, keeping the root intact. Put them in a bowl, drizzle with a couple of tablespoons of olive oil, and sprinkle with some salt and pepper. Mix well, then put them in a roasting tray (this keeps most of the oil on the onions and not all over the tray, where it will burn) and roast in the oven for 40 minutes.

While the shallots are in the oven, put a frying pan over a medium-low heat, add the diced chorizo and a tablespoon of olive oil and fry for 2–3 minutes until lightly browned and cooked through. Add the thyme sprigs just before the chorizo's ready. Set aside and warm through again before serving.

Heat the remaining 3 tablespoons of the olive oil in a large saucepan over a medium heat. Add the lemon zest, fennel seeds and garlic and cook for 2–3 minutes, stirring constantly. Tip in the beans and the liquid from the tins, the stock and wine and bring to the boil, then reduce the heat and simmer for 5 minutes, stirring occasionally. You just want to cook it long enough to burn off the alcohol and make sure everyone is getting along – the starch in the bean liquor will have made the sauce creamy and we want the beans to have a good texture. Turn off the heat and stir through the lemon juice and grated cheese. Finish with the roasted shallots, and the chorizo and its frying oil poured over the top, and sprinkle with parsley. I always have extra lemon wedges for squeezing ready as well.

ONIONS LEEKS AUBERGINES MUSHROOMS

My mom's relatives were from Sicily, and the way I make this dish sits somewhere between her method and how I had it on holiday on the island of Pantelleria (between Sicily and Tunisia) a few years ago. The sauce is agrodolce – sour and sweet – and is often served with pine nuts and raisins, which is not really my vibe. I use tomato purée and wine but passata is more traditional. I love it when dishes hit all these notes to make a perfectly balanced flavour. Caponata is usually served as a snack with drinks, but it's a main event for me. Serve with dry, crusty bread to soak up the sauce.

caponata

SERVES **2–3** AS A MAIN DISH

extra virgin olive oil, for frying
1 large aubergine or 2 smaller aubergines, diced
1 fennel bulb, trimmed and thinly sliced
200g cherry tomatoes, halved
2 large onions, thinly sliced
4–6 celery stalks, thinly sliced
100g double-concentrated tomato purée
230ml dry white wine
4 tbsp capers, drained
150g green olives, pitted
3 tbsp white wine vinegar
1 tsp dried red chilli flakes (or more if you prefer it hotter – I do)
1–2 tbsp caster sugar
salt and pepper
toasted bread, for dipping and scooping

Heat the oil in a wide frying pan or casserole dish over a medium heat (you want to heat enough oil to cover the aubergine), then add the aubergine and fry for about 6 minutes until lightly golden. It can seem a bit extra to cover them in oil here, but the flavour and texture you get from frying an aubergine are very unique and important to this dish. Once lightly golden, remove with a slotted spoon, transfer to a paper towel to soak up excess oil and season with salt.

Using 2 tablespoons of the aubergine frying oil (strain and keep the rest for future use), sauté the fennel, cherry tomatoes, onions and celery in the same pan over a medium heat for about 10 minutes until soft. Add the tomato purée and wine and cook over a medium heat until the wine has reduced by half. Add the capers, olives, fried aubergine, vinegar, chilli flakes, a generous pinch of black pepper and the sugar (to taste).

Check before seasoning with salt – it should be salty enough from the olives and capers. Serve with lots of toasted bread and enjoy.

ONIONS LEEKS AUBERGINES MUSHROOMS

When I'm feeling like a hungry kid, grilled cheese usually comes to mind. It's important to let your inner kid be part of your cooking to keep things indulgent, exciting and just plain good. I love a crunchy-soggy combination, and when this grilled cheese is dipped into a consommé it really satisfies the craving for that experience. I use a beef consommé but a vegetable broth with a generous splash of soy sauce would be great as well.

french onion grilled cheese with consommé

MAKES **2** BIG-BOY GRILLED CHEESES

50g unsalted butter, plus extra for spreading

1 thyme sprig

4–6 white onions, thinly sliced

2 garlic cloves, grated

1 tbsp balsamic vinegar

1 tbsp Worcestershire sauce

4 slices white sourdough

100–150g Gruyère cheese, grated (split 50/50 with grated mature Cheddar for a milder flavour)

300ml beef consommé, bone broth, or vegetable broth with soy sauce, for dipping

salt

Put the butter and thyme in a large saucepan over a medium-low heat and when the butter has melted add the thinly sliced onions and garlic. Cook for 40 minutes, stirring frequently and seasoning with salt about halfway through. If it looks like the onions are starting to brown too fast or burn, turn down the heat and add a splash of water. You will most likely have to add about 5 splashes of water over the 40-minute period to keep things under control. I don't like to add the vinegar or Worcestershire sauce until the colour of the onions is looking right – they will throw that off right away – so add them around the 40-minute mark, when everything is starting to look brown and jammy. Cook for another 20 minutes or until the liquid has almost all evaporated. You need enough liquid to mix with the fat – if the fat is separating from the onions add a little splash of water to bring it back together. The onions should be completely tender and a bit of a flavour bomb. Taste them and if you want them sweeter add a pinch of sugar (or a little splash of vinegar if they are too sweet and need a little balance in the other direction).

A good grilled cheese needs time and weight. Generously butter all slices of bread on both sides, then add an even layer of the onion mix to two slices, followed by the cheese, then more onion. Close the sandwiches and cook in a heavy-based frying pan over a medium-low heat for 5–7 minutes on each side with a weight on top, such as another pan (just make sure it's not too big as you don't want to create any steam). By the time it's ready it should be flatter, deeply golden, and the cheese should have totally melted into the onions. If you're going for the dip, make sure it's hot and ready and that it's well seasoned, otherwise it could dilute the flavours you've worked so hard for.

I don't mind enduring long, cold and grey days in London as long as I can have dishes like this. It tastes like it has been bubbling away for hours but comes together quickly. Cooking the leeks in two stages makes them incredibly tender – almost as if they had been stewed – with a sweet, caramelised exterior. The salsa verde is optional if you want to keep things simple, but I recommend adding it to cut through the richness and give your meal a little bright green pop.

tender leeks, beans and salsa verde

SERVES 2

2 large leeks
2 tbsp extra virgin olive oil
½ lemon
75g smoked pancetta, diced
4 garlic cloves, thinly sliced
250ml dry white wine
400g tin cannellini beans
   (with tin liquid)
1 tbsp crème fraîche
salt and pepper

FOR THE SALSA VERDE
(OPTIONAL)

handful of parsley
handful of mint
handful of chives
100g tin anchovy fillets in oil
1½ tsp Dijon mustard
1 tbsp white wine vinegar
juice of ½ lemon
3 tbsp extra virgin olive oil

Remove the first 2 or 3 layers from the leeks and trim the tops and bottoms before cutting them in half widthways, then cutting them lengthways in half. Steam for 8 minutes, then transfer to a well-seasoned ice bath to cool. Pat the leeks dry with a clean tea towel.

Heat the oil in a frying pan over a high heat and add the steamed leeks, flipping them when they have a good amount of colour and are just shy of burning. Season with salt and a squeeze of lemon juice.

Fry the pancetta and garlic in the olive oil in a frying pan over a medium heat for a few minutes, until the garlic has softened and the pancetta is starting to brown, then add the white wine and beans (with their liquid). Simmer for 10 minutes, then finish with the crème fraîche, another squeeze of lemon juice and some black pepper.

While the beans are simmering, blitz the ingredients for the salsa verde (if using) in a food processor till relatively smooth and warm through the leeks in a pan if necessary. Season to taste.

Plate the beans, add the warmed leeks and top with the salsa verde.

The combination of char and steam transforms a leek into a truly unique textural and taste experience – tender and sweet, with an earthy umami. All you need to do is throw the leek on some hot coals and let it burn all over – the heat from the coal does the rest of the work. I love leeks cooked like this so much that I often think about different ways to build a meal around them. I think that this particular combination could be my favourite. The first time I had whipped cod's roe was at St John in London – smoked fish eggs that had been whipped into a rich, airy sauce. I ordered a second plate after the first bite and never looked back. The flavour is too good to ever really get a hold of, it just keeps growing and I keep chasing, slightly dazed by the time I've finished.

grilled leeks and whipped cod's roe

SERVES **4** (FOR SHARING)

4–6 leeks
salt
Quick Pickled Chilli (page 31),
  chopped, to serve

FOR THE WHIPPED COD'S ROE

125g smoked cod's roe
2 garlic cloves, peeled
2g white peppercorns
grated zest and juice of
  1 lemon
10ml white wine vinegar
50g ice cubes
500ml rapeseed oil

Put all the ingredients for the whipped cod's roe, except the oil, in a blender and blend until smooth, scraping down the sides as you go. With the blender on medium speed, slowly add the oil through the funnel, like you would when making a mayonnaise or dressing, until it is all incorporated and the mixture is thick and spreadable. Keep the whipped cod's roe in the fridge – you'll need to take it out about 15 minutes before serving, so it's not too cold.

Add the leeks directly to hot-white smouldering coals and leave to char all over for 10–15 minutes. When finished they should be soft to the touch and black all over. Leave to rest until cool enough to handle. Remove the burnt outer layer and trim the top and bottom.

I like to have the leeks warm or hot with the cool whipped cod's roe. You can quickly heat them in a hot pan if you've grilled them ahead of time, or put them in the microwave for 30 seconds. Spread the cod's roe over your plate and lay the leeks on top, finishing the dish with a little salt and some chopped pickled chilli.

Labneh spaghetti is a Lebanese dish that is simple and incredibly tasty. Celebrating beautiful labneh with the addition of garlic and za'atar, this version also incorporates confit leeks – the rest of the method I believe is pretty classic (how I've been shown to make it). Confit leeks are a great item to have on hand and the leftover oil is full of flavour, so don't discard it – keep it and use it to finish other dishes and vinaigrettes.

leek confit and labneh spaghetti

SERVES 2

4 leeks, topped and tailed
 and halved lengthways
6 garlic cloves, 4 peeled and
 left whole, 2 sliced
300ml olive oil (or a neutral
 oil like rapeseed)
3 tbsp labneh
200g dried spaghetti
juice of ½ lemon
za'atar, to taste
salt and pepper

Remove and discard the dirty outer layers of the leek halves (you can rinse them and keep them for making stock), rinse in cold water, then cut into 2cm lengths. Put them in a saucepan with 4 peeled garlic cloves and enough oil to just cover, then cook over a low heat for 1 hour. If you don't want to leave them on the hob, you can transfer them to an ovenproof dish that's small enough for the oil to cover the leeks and garlic, then put them in the oven at 150°C fan and cook for 1–2 hours.

The garlic and leeks should be golden brown and tender. Remove from the heat (or the oven) and leave to cool before straining, making sure to save the oil in a jar.

Put the leeks and garlic in a blender with a tablespoon of the cooking oil, the labneh, a pinch of salt and a splash of water, then blend until smooth.

Get the spaghetti cooking in salted boiling water. Halfway through its cooking time, put the thinly sliced garlic into a frying pan with 3 tablespoons of the leek confit oil and cook over a medium-high heat until the garlic is golden. Transfer the pasta straight from the water into the frying pan (using tongs) with a few spoonfuls of the pasta cooking water and the leek and labneh purée and stir to combine. It should form a creamy sauce that clings to all the pasta – if it is too thick, keep adding pasta water. Remove from the heat and finish with the lemon juice and lots of za'atar.

ONIONS LEEKS AUBERGINES MUSHROOMS

There are almost always leeks in my house. I'm not always 100 per cent sure how they get there, but I have cooked with them in every style I can think of. This is relatively quick and easy, but feels comforting in the way that something that took hours to make does.

leek gratin

SERVES 2–3

4 leeks, trimmed, halved
    lengthways and washed
1 tbsp plain flour
1 tbsp unsalted butter
300ml whole milk
1 garlic clove, grated with a
    microplane grater
1 tbsp Dijon mustard
100g mature Cheddar
    cheese, grated
50g panko breadcrumbs
1 rosemary sprig, leaves
    stripped and finely chopped
grated zest of I lemon
2 tbsp extra virgin olive oil
salt and pepper

Preheat the oven to 200°C fan.

Steam the leeks for 7 minutes.

While the leeks are steaming, put the flour and butter in a saucepan over a medium heat and whisk for 3–4 minutes until combined and lightly golden. Gradually add the milk, whisking continuously. When all the milk is incorporated and there are no lumps, add the grated garlic, mustard and cheese. Cook for another minute or two, stirring until the cheese is melted and you have a smooth sauce. Taste and check for seasoning before adding salt and pepper.

Put the breadcrumbs, chopped rosemary and lemon zest in a frying pan with the olive oil and toast over a medium heat for a few minutes until lightly golden.

Place the leeks, cut side up, in a baking tray or oven dish, ideally one that can accommodate them in a single layer. Spread the cheese sauce over evenly, then add the toasted breadcrumbs.

Bake in the oven for 10 minutes, until the cheese sauce is bubbling and the breadcrumbs are golden.

I like to serve this with lightly dressed gem lettuce and quick-pickled onions, preparing the onions by simply adding some nice vinegar and a little sugar to some sliced onion and chilli.

If I'm going to go through the process of charring aubergines for any dish, I'll normally char a couple extra and keep the flesh for this ragout (you can also freeze it). It really takes the ragout to another level, adding a ton of bass, like Pink Floyd's Money-level bass. Leave out the lentils and you have an amazing pasta sauce, add some capers and olives to that sauce and you can spoon it over grilled fish, or – one of my favourites – add it to a lasagne. Unreal.

smoky aubergine and lentil ragout

SERVES 4

3–4 tbsp extra virgin olive oil (enough to coat the bottom of the pan), plus extra for drizzling
4 garlic cloves, thinly sliced
1 carrot, finely diced
2 onions, finely diced
1 celery stalk, finely diced
1 tsp dried red chilli flakes
130g tube of tomato purée (double- or triple-concentrated)
250ml stock (I use chicken because it's what I normally have on hand, but vegetable stock or water works)
250ml dry white wine
200g dried green lentils, rinsed and drained
cooked flesh of 3–4 charred aubergines (page 229)
salt and pepper

TO SERVE

4 generous tbsp labneh
handful of parsley, roughly chopped

Heat the oil in a large, tall-sided sauté pan or casserole dish over a medium heat, then add the garlic, carrot, onions, celery and chilli flakes and cook for about 10 minutes until softened but not browned.

Push the veggies to one side and shift the pan or dish so they are not on the heat (or remove them from the pan entirely). Add the tomato purée to the hot spot, stirring continuously – it will start to caramelise and almost burn, adding a ton of flavour. After a few minutes (put the veggies back in if you removed them) add the stock, wine and lentils. Bring to the boil, then reduce the heat and simmer, covered, for 20 minutes.

Add the aubergine flesh, season with salt and pepper, and cook uncovered for a further 5–10 minutes, until the lentils are tender and the sauce is thick.

Serve with a big scoop of labneh, lots of parsley and some good extra virgin olive oil.

This is basically an aubergine parmigiana, a classic I have love for but don't really get down with these days. I usually want it to taste more like aubergine, with a bit of crunch, and have something bright and acidic to cut through it beyond the tomato sauce. This has a deep smoky aubergine flavour and a whole lot of texture from the softest to the crunchiest side of the spectrum: it is very similar to aubergine parm on paper but it's a totally different experience.

smoky aubergine parm

SERVES **2** (GENEROUSLY)

2 aubergines
50g plain flour
1 egg, lightly beaten with
   120ml milk
100g panko breadcrumbs
neutral oil, for shallow-frying
   (I use rapeseed)
100g burrata
handful of parsley
handful of basil
1 tbsp Quick Pickled Chilli
   (see page 31)
1 tsp white wine vinegar
salt and pepper

FOR THE CONFIT GARLIC

1 bulb garlic, cloves peeled
enough neutral oil to cover

FOR THE SAUCE

bunch of basil
1 tbsp extra virgin olive oil
250g cherry tomatoes
2 shallots, thinly sliced
6 cloves confit garlic
1 tbsp white wine vinegar
1 tsp caster sugar

First confit the garlic. Add the garlic cloves to a saucepan with enough oil to cover, then cook over a low heat for 30 minutes.

Char the aubergines over a flame following the method on page 229. While they are cooking, lightly fry the basil in the olive oil for about 30 seconds over a medium-high heat then remove – set aside to add back to the sauce later. Turn up the heat, add the tomatoes and cook for 5 minutes until lightly blistered. Turn the heat down to medium and add the shallots. When the shallots have softened, add the 6 cloves confit garlic and carefully smash them along with the tomatoes with the back of your spatula or spoon. Add the vinegar, sugar and some salt and pepper and cook for about a minute, then set aside.

Gently press the aubergine flesh into a flattened pear shape and season with salt and pepper. Set up your pané station. You can use three shallow trays or bowls: one with flour, one with beaten egg, and one with breadcrumbs. Carefully dredge the aubergines in the egg, then the flour and breadcrumbs.

Shallow fry the coated aubergines in a sauté pan over a high heat until golden brown on both sides. Do this at a relatively high temperature – the aubergine is cooked and the faster the crust develops the less oil it will absorb. Bake the aubergine in the oven if you prefer: lightly coat it with olive oil and bake at 220°C fan until golden on both sides (flipping them mid bake). Remove the aubergine from the pan or oven. Season with salt.

Add the basil to the warm sauce. Top the sauce with the crunchy aubergine, tear over the burrata and garnish with the herbs, vinegar and pickled chilli.

227

ONIONS LEEKS AUBERGINES MUSHROOMS

Like many fried foods, this fried aubergine dish can easily morph from one flavour to another. Of all the versions I've tried, this one is a very close second to my Smoky Aubergine Parm (page 226). Tonkatsu (fried pork cutlet with shredded cabbage and barbecue sauce) is a completely perfect meal for me. It's so simple and it has a lovely balance and texture of flavour – tender meat, crunchy golden breadcrumb crust, freshness from the cabbage and a sweet tangy sauce with a whole lot of body. The aubergine slotted into the dish perfectly. Tonkatsu is essentially a Japanese fruit-based barbecue sauce, and it's fun to make, but shop-bought sauce from Asian grocers is totally delicious too (I use the Bulldog brand).

aubergine katsu

SERVES 2

½ head white cabbage
2 aubergines
50g plain flour
1 egg, lightly beaten with
    120ml milk
100g panko breadcrumbs
neutral oil, for shallow-frying
    (I use rapeseed)
lemon slices, to serve

FOR THE TONKATSU SAUCE

50g demerara sugar
200g tomato ketchup
200ml red wine
1 plum or peach, stoned and
    roughly chopped (dried
    fruits like dates or figs are
    good too)
4 tbsp Worcestershire sauce
4 tbsp light soy sauce
4 tbsp rice vinegar
1 generous tsp Marmite

Thinly slice the cabbage using a mandoline. Put it in a bowl of iced water for 2 minutes, then drain and leave to dry on a clean towel while you prepare the sauce. The iced water enhances the cabbage's crunch and gives it extra volume.

To make your own tonkatsu sauce, put all the ingredients in a saucepan and bring to the boil, then reduce the heat and simmer for 15 minutes. Pass through a sieve and leave to cool at room temperature.

Pierce a few shallow holes in the aubergines with the tip of a knife then cook over an open flame, rotating the aubergines every 3–4 minutes, or under a hot oven grill for 20 minutes, flipping them halfway through. They should be completely charred on all sides and the inside should be soft. Transfer to a bowl, cover tightly with a lid or cling film and leave to steam and cool for 5 minutes. Remove the burnt skin from the aubergines, keeping the aubergines as one piece: I like to use a paper towel to wipe away all the smaller pieces of char.

Gently press the aubergine flesh into a flattened pear shape and season with salt and pepper. Set up your pané station. You can use three shallow trays or bowls: one with flour, one with beaten egg and milk, and one with breadcrumbs. Carefully dredge the aubergines in the egg, then the flour and breadcrumbs.
continued overleaf...

aubergine katsu *(continued)*

Shallow fry the coated aubergines in a sauté pan or frying pan over a high heat until golden brown on both sides. It's best to do this at a relatively high temperature – the aubergine is already cooked and the faster the crust develops the less oil it will absorb. You could bake the aubergine in the oven if you prefer: lightly coat it with olive oil and bake at 220°C fan until golden brown on both sides (flipping them mid bake).

Warm the sauce through, if necessary, then spoon a generous amount of the warm sauce onto a plate and place the crispy aubergine on top. Add a big handful of the shredded cabbage and serve with slices of lemon.

Once you've learned to cook an aubergine over an open flame (like in the Smoky Aubergine Parm recipe on page 226 and Baba Ganoush recipe on page 188) a whole world of possibilities opens up. One of my favourite ways to eat smoky aubergine is in this bánh mì-style sandwich. You can also flex your 3-2-1 pickling skills (see page 31) to prepare pickled carrots and daikon. It's a seriously punchy combination of flavours and textures.

smoked aubergine bánh mì

SERVES 2

1 carrot, peeled and cut into julienne (thin strips)
piece of daikon, peeled and cut into julienne (thin strips)
3-2-1 pickling liquid (see page 31)
2 aubergines
1 lemongrass stalk, outer layer removed, stem trimmed and stalk roughly chopped
thumb-sized piece of ginger, peeled and roughly chopped
1 garlic clove, chopped
1 or 2 Thai chillies, chopped
1 tbsp roughly chopped coriander stems
1 tsp dried chilli flakes
2 tsp fish sauce
juice of 1 lime
1 tbsp caster sugar

TO SERVE

2 bánh mì rolls or a sub sandwich roll
mayonnaise
cucumber, sliced
fresh jalapeño, sliced
coriander leaves, torn
mint leaves, torn
shop-bought crispy shallots

Put the carrot and daikon strips in a heatproof bowl, then cover with boiling 3-2-1 pickling liquid (three parts vinegar, two parts water and one part sugar). Leave in the fridge to cool for at least a couple of hours, then they are good to go.

Start by piercing a few shallow holes in the aubergines with the tip of a knife, then cook over an open flame, rotating the aubergines every 3–4 minutes, or under a hot oven grill for 20 minutes, flipping them halfway through. They should be completely charred on all sides and the inside should be soft. Transfer to a bowl, cover tightly with a lid or cling film and leave to steam and cool for 5 minutes. Remove the burnt skin from the aubergines: I like to use a paper towel to wipe away all the smaller pieces of char. Trim off the stems and roughly chop the flesh – you should be left with a soft smoky mix that's ready for seasoning.

Put the roughly chopped lemongrass, ginger, garlic, Thai chillies and coriander stems in a mortar. Add the chilli flakes, fish sauce, lime juice and sugar and pound with the pestle until you have a cohesive paste. The more you work it the better – work it, you're worth it.

Add the mix one spoonful at a time to the aubergine and stir well. It should taste pretty punchy, but you can stop adding it when you're happy.

Now, build the sandwiches: spread the mayo in the bánh mì rolls, then add the smoked aubergine, followed by the cucumber, jalapeño, pickled carrots and daikon, coriander, mint and crispy shallots.

When you start using crispy polenta as a bed for food, a new chapter will begin in your life. This is a seriously cosy meal, perfect for those cold, dark nights with a generous glass of red wine. If you can, use a mix of wild mushrooms. If not, try to use a mix that has a little character, varied in shapes, shades and sizes. This dish is great served with a butterhead lettuce salad dressed with Dijon vinaigrette. Crispy polenta is made in the same way as panisse (chickpea frites). They are often served as perfect deep-fried planks, but recently I have been introduced to the roughly cut slab of polenta that's shallow-fried or baked, and it's a beautiful thing. It's such an easy way to have a different version of a golden, crispy starch at the table.

mushrooms and crispy polenta

SERVES 2–3

50g smoked bacon lardons
   (optional)
2 tbsp extra virgin olive oil
2 thyme sprigs
2 garlic cloves, finely
   chopped
1 onion, finely chopped
400g mixed mushrooms
   (or any mushroom you
   prefer), halved or roughly
   chopped (keep some whole
   if possible)
100ml dry white wine
100ml chicken stock
1 tbsp Dijon mustard
50g crème fraîche
50g Gruyère cheese, grated
1 tbsp white wine vinegar
2 tbsp cold butter, diced
   (optional)
salt and pepper
handful of parsley, to serve

FOR THE CRISPY POLENTA

250ml whole milk
250ml water
50g unsalted butter
300g coarse polenta
1 tsp cayenne pepper
neutral oil (such as rapeseed),
   for frying and greasing the
   tray

First, prepare the polenta. Bring the liquids and butter to a simmer in a large saucepan over a medium heat, then slowly add the polenta while stirring constantly. Add the cayenne and some salt and pepper and keep stirring over a medium-low heat for about 10 minutes until the mixture is thick and softened.

Rub a baking tray with oil, then add the polenta. If you want it smooth and even, grease the bottom of another tray and use it to press out the mixture. Otherwise, just use a spatula to spread it out into a roughly even layer, then leave it to cool for a few hours in the fridge.

Put the lardons (if using), oil, thyme, garlic, onion and mushrooms in a large saucepan or casserole dish over a medium heat and cook for 30 minutes, or until the mushrooms have browned, stirring often. Season with salt and pepper, then deglaze with the white wine. Add the stock and cook for another 10 minutes, then add the mustard, crème fraîche and grated cheese and cook for another couple of minutes. Add the vinegar to bring the sauce together, and check for seasoning.

Cut or break the chilled polenta into big squares, then pan-fry in a generous amount of oil over a medium-high heat for about 4 minutes on each side until crispy on all sides. Alternatively, brush the pieces with oil and roast on a lined baking tray at 220°C fan for about 30 minutes, flipping them halfway through.

I like to stir cold pieces of butter through the mushroom mixture just before spooning it over the crispy polenta. Finish the dish with a generous amount of chopped or whole parsley.

As you know, I am from LA, arguably the birthplace of 'fusion' cooking, and although much good has come of the combination of Southeast Asian and European ingredients, quite a lot of not-so-good has too. There is a line between blending different cultures' ingredients respectfully and being a douche and I hope I don't land on the wrong side of it with this one. The salad is extremely tasty, and I love to eat it too much not to include it.

soba noodle salad

SERVES 2

25g dried wood ear mushrooms or Chinese black fungus
200g buckwheat soba noodles
1 red pepper, deseeded and cut into julienne (thin strips)
½ cucumber, deseeded and cut into julienne (thin strips)
1 carrot, peeled and cut into julienne (thin strips)
1 red chilli, cut into julienne (thin strips)
handful of coriander, finely chopped
4 spring onions, trimmed and thinly sliced
1 tbsp toasted sesame seeds

FOR THE DRESSING

20g sweet white miso paste
40g tahini
10g brown sugar or honey
25ml rice vinegar
1 tbsp sriracha, or to taste
1 tbsp toasted sesame oil
10g fresh ginger, peeled
30ml water

Put the dried mushrooms in a heatproof bowl, cover with boiling water and leave to soak for 15 minutes. Once hydrated, drain, trim the stems and rinse off any dirt or debris, then cut into thin strips.

Cook the noodles according to the packet instructions, then cool them under cold running water in a colander or sieve. Set aside to dry.

Put the dressing ingredients in a blender and blend until smooth, adding a little extra water to loosen it if it's too thick.

Put all the salad ingredients in a bowl, including the mushrooms and noodles, and reserving some herbs, sesame seeds and vegetables to garnish. Mix the dressing through and adjust the seasoning. if it's too thick add a little water, and add a pinch of salt or some vinegar if you want it to be a little sharper. Garnish with the remaining herbs, vegetables and seeds.

a few sweet things

When I was growing up in California, the only popsicle (ice lolly) in an ice cream truck that had any real fruit in it was a paleta. It wasn't my first choice as a kid, as I would usually go for something with a nuclear green hue, but once my friends put me onto them, I found myself starting to order them most of the time. Especially when I discovered how much I loved the combination of sweet, savoury and spicy. Mango and chamoy (a fruity Mexican hot sauce), usually called mangonada, became my go-to combination and it's still very much my favourite: add some chamoy, a fruit-based hot sauce, to the mix below if you want to try it. I love putting paletas on a menu as they are fun to eat and such a refreshing and delicious way to end a meal.

mango and sour cherry paletas

MAKES 6-8

500g diced frozen or fresh mango
100g caster sugar
6 limes, 4 for juicing, the rest sliced to serve
125g maraschino cherries, drained
chamoy sauce, to taste (optional)
tajin (Mexican chilli and lime seasoning), to taste (optional)

Put the frozen mango and sugar in a large saucepan over a medium heat. When the sugar has dissolved and the mango has started to soften, transfer to a blender with the lime juice and blitz until smooth.

Rinse out the blender, blitz half the cherries until smooth, then mix them with the remaining whole cherries.

Fill 6–8 individual lolly moulds quarter-full with the mango mixture, add a few spoons of the cherry mix and marble in the chamoy sauce (if using), then top up with the mango. Use a toothpick to gently swirl the mix, creating a marbled effect. If you don't have a lolly-mould holder with stick inserts attached to the lid, leave them to set in the freezer for 30 minutes before adding the popsicle sticks. Freeze for at least 12 hours.

I like to serve them with a slice of lime and some tajin.

I am, to all intents and purposes, a stray. I moved to London when I was 20, only knowing one person. Having a family home to visit, for no other reason than you wanted to, was something I dearly missed. The Standings' family home became that place for me, and Sarah – the incredible matriarch – and I connected over our love of food. I learned so much from her cooking – I loved the way she could casually throw a perfect pudding together, in the way that a mama does, and this is her recipe.

sarah's pomegranate and orange pudding

SERVES 6

100g ground almonds
175g soft light brown sugar
2 tsp baking powder
50g homemade wholemeal
  breadcrumbs
finely grated zest of
  3 oranges, plus extra
  to serve
215ml olive oil
4 eggs, lightly beaten
seeds from 1 pomegranate,
  plus extra to serve

FOR THE SYRUP

2 tbsp runny honey, plus extra
  for drizzling
juice of 1 orange
100ml pure pomegranate
  juice
1 tbsp pomegranate molasses

TO SERVE

mint leaves
thick Greek yoghurt
shelled unsalted pistachios,
  roughly chopped

Grease a 20cm springform cake tin with olive oil.

To make the sponge, mix the dry ingredients together, then combine them with wet (including the orange zest and pomegranate seeds) and pour into the greased tin. Put into a cold oven and turn the heat to 190°C fan.

Bake for 50 minutes, or until a knife inserted into the middle of the cake comes out clean.

To make the syrup, put the honey, juices and molasses in a saucepan and heat gently until the honey has melted into the juice, then simmer for about 5 minutes.

When the sponge is cooked, remove it from the oven, make a lot of little holes in the surface and pour the syrup over it (while it's still in the tin). When cooled, turn it out (carefully, as it will be moist and wobbly).

Pile pomegranate seeds in the middle with some more orange zest and some fresh mint leaves.

Sarah serves it with thick Greek yoghurt drizzled with honey and sprinkled with pistachios, revealing their green interiors. The pudding is best served on the day but does keep for 2–3 days covered in the fridge.

My wife's sister, Olivia, is the flip side to me – I don't think I have ever seen her cook a savoury meal, but she can bake absolutely anything, and her cake and biscuit decorating skills are next level. This is a simple and perfect dinner party dessert and it actually doesn't require any baking at all, it is all just assembling and refrigerating, but it looks fancy AF. You need to make it at least 5–6 hours ahead of serving.

olivia's white chocolate cheesecake

SERVES 6–8

300g ginger biscuits
120g melted unsalted butter, for the biscuit base
500g good-quality white chocolate (not baking chocolate), broken into pieces
250g mascarpone
250g full-fat cream cheese
juice of 1 lemon, or to taste
fruit, to serve (something tart and not too sweet, like redcurrants or passion fruit)

Line the base of a 20cm springform cake tin with baking parchment.

Blitz the ginger biscuits in a blender until they form crumbs, then transfer them to a mixing bowl. Pour the melted butter slowly onto the crushed biscuits and mix by hand until they are all stuck together. Tip the biscuit mix into the lined tin and press it down firmly. Put in the fridge to chill for a couple of hours.

Melt the white chocolate using a bain-marie or in a microwave-safe bowl in the microwave in short bursts, then allow it to cool down a little. In a separate bowl, whisk the mascarpone and cream cheese until totally blended. Add the melted white chocolate and thoroughly mix through, adding some lemon juice to take the edge off the sweetness. Pour the white chocolate and cheese mix over the chilled biscuit base and gently smooth the surface. Cover the cake tin with cling film and chill in the fridge overnight, or for a minimum of 5–6 hours.

Serve with a dollop of fruit on top – something sharp like passion fruit or redcurrants.

Every Friday my mother-in-law Diane looks after our three-year-old son Hamilton until I collect him at 2pm and every week they bake a cake together. Their ritual is to walk to the shops to buy the fruit – which Hamilton selects – but the rest of the recipe stays the same. They eat about a quarter of it and then he brings the rest home for us.

Diane and Hamilton have made this cake with apricots, blueberries, cranberries, peaches and rhubarb –they all work. My favourite to come home with is one made with plums or apricots. It is a failsafe cake to serve for Sunday afternoon tea and looks pretty enough to serve as dessert with a scoop of crème fraîche or ice cream.

friday cake for hamilton

SERVES 6–8

125g unsalted butter,
  softened
2 eggs
150g caster sugar
150g plain flour
1 tsp bicarbonate of soda
1 tsp ground cinnamon (Diane
  said she just shakes it in
  until she likes the colour)
150g cornmeal, polenta or
  rolled oats
250g natural yoghurt
500g apricots or plums,
  pitted and quartered
crème fraîche, to serve

Preheat the oven to 180°C fan and line the base and sides of a 23cm round cake tin with baking parchment.

Mix the softened butter, eggs and sugar together in a bowl with a whisk to combine.

Gradually add the flour, bicarbonate of soda and cinnamon along with the cornmeal, polenta or oats, then gently mix in the yoghurt until incorporated. Fold in whatever fruit you're using (be careful not to over-mix the batter) or line the cake tin with the fruit in a sort of upside-down cake way.

Transfer the batter to the cake tin and bake for 45–60 minutes, until the top is springy and a knife inserted into the middle of the cake comes out clean. Put a layer of foil on top for the last 15 minutes if you're worried it's burning.

Remove from the oven and let it cool in the tin, then turn it out carefully onto a plate and eat. Preferably with crème fraîche.

My great pal Anna Greenland is an organic vegetable grower who lives in Suffolk in a converted threshing barn with her awesome husband Hugo and two girls. They are the sort of people you would want to be hunkered down with for the apocalypse – they built their house basically themselves and live as much as possible off their land.

From a distance, Anna might appear whimsical as she wears floaty clothes and speaks gently, but she is as tough as a pirate and much funnier. Her depth of knowledge about vegetables and growing is wild (she has been the head grower for several famous chefs and restaurants). Cooking with Anna at her house means going outside and digging something up or cutting it off a stalk to prepare, or often eating it immediately, which makes me happier than I can say.

This is a beautiful rich chocolate beetroot cake Anna made us all last time we were there and so I asked if I could put it in this book for you all.

chocolate beetroot cake

SERVES **8–10**

250g raw beetroot, peeled
   and cut into cubes
200g unsalted butter, cubed,
   plus extra for greasing
200g dark chocolate, broken
   into pieces
250g coconut sugar
5 eggs
1 tsp vanilla extract
240g ground almonds
1 tsp baking powder
pinch of salt
crème fraîche, to serve
   (optional, but nice)

Preheat the oven to 170°C fan and grease and line a 23cm round cake tin with baking parchment.

Steam the cubed beetroot for about 30 minutes, then allow to cool a little.

Melt the butter and chocolate together gently in a saucepan, turning off the heat when everything is liquid. Leave to cool a bit before mixing with anything else, so the eggs don't start to cook when they go together.

Blitz the steamed and cooled beetroot in a food processor until smooth, then add the coconut sugar and blitz again. Add the eggs one at a time, blitzing between additions, then transfer the mix to a bowl and stir through the cooled melted chocolate and butter. Add the vanilla, then add the ground almonds, baking powder and salt, fold through and pour into your lined cake tin.

Bake for 20 minutes, then turn the oven temperature down to 160°C fan and bake for a further 20 minutes, until a knife inserted into the middle of the cake comes out clean.

Remove from the oven and leave to cool in the tin before slicing.

My wife's grandmother – known to everyone as Babe since she was a little girl – has been making this apple cake since the 1950s in Ohio, and Diane, my mother-in-law, has been making it since she moved to England in the 80s, so it was a staple of Francesca's childhood. There are never any leftovers for the next day; it is very good and pretty foolproof (I am the fool here). We make it in a 24cm bundt cake tin and dust it with icing sugar just before serving.

babe's apple cake

SERVES 12–16

240ml rapeseed oil, plus extra
  for greasing
220g caster sugar
3 eggs
1½ tsp ground cinnamon
1 tsp bicarbonate of soda
½ tsp fine salt
250g plain flour, plus extra for
  dusting
150g walnuts, coarsely
  chopped
240g dessert apples, peeled,
  cored and cut into thin-ish
  slices
icing sugar, for dusting

Preheat the oven to 180°C fan. Grease a 24cm bundt tin with oil and dust with flour.

Mix the rapeseed oil and caster sugar together in a mixing bowl, then stir through the eggs followed by your cinnamon, bicarbonate of soda and salt. Sift the flour into the batter with a fine-mesh sieve, then gently fold through the nuts and apples.

Pour the mixture into the prepared tin and bake in the oven for 35–45 minutes, or until a knife inserted into the sponge comes out clean.

Remove from the oven and leave to cool in the tin before turning out onto a wire rack or serving plate.

Dust with icing sugar using a fine-mesh sieve just before serving.

At the time I am writing this book Babe – my wife's grandma – is 92 years old. Since I met Francesca eight years ago, we have made an annual visit to Babe in New Smyrna Beach, Florida, making it our big family holiday with the kids. Babe always makes an absolute pile of these before we come, and they live in her big American fridge in the garage. We mostly enter and exit the house through her garage and Francesca and I almost can't walk past it without popping one of these little squares in our mouths. We have just learned to make them ourselves, so I can guarantee they will now be a family staple and hopefully something we will be baking for our own greedy grandkids one day.

three-layer brownie confections

MAKES 10–12

FIRST LAYER – BROWNIE BASE

150g unsalted butter, plus
  extra for greasing
140g dark cooking chocolate,
  broken into pieces (as
  unsweetened as you can
  find)
280g granulated sugar
2 tsp vanilla extract
3 eggs
125g plain flour

SECOND LAYER – WHITE ICING

80g unsalted butter
240g icing sugar
3 tbsp milk
1 tsp vanilla extract

THIRD LAYER – CHOCOLATE

40g dark cooking chocolate,
  broken into pieces
2 tbsp unsalted butter

Brownie base

Preheat the oven to 180°C fan and grease the base and sides of a 23cm square cake tin.

Melt the butter and chocolate in a saucepan over a low heat, stirring constantly, then take off the heat and let it cool slightly. In the bowl of a stand mixer fitted with the beater attachment beat the sugar, vanilla and eggs on high speed, then turn the speed down to low and beat in the chocolate mixture. Stir in the flour by hand, then spread the batter out in your cake tin.

Bake the brownie base in the oven for 40–45 minutes, or just until the brownie begins to pull away from the edges of the tin. Remove from the oven and let the brownie cool completely in the tin on a wire rack, then turn out onto a flat surface for the next step. We are going to leave it upside down like this, so the top is perfectly flat for icing.

Second layer

Melt the butter in a saucepan nearly to the point of it darkening in colour, when the solids separate from the fat, then turn off the heat. Mix in the icing sugar and then the milk and vanilla. Frost the (completely cooled down) brownie with this white icing all over, then put it in the fridge.

Third layer

When the white icing layer is cool and hardened, gently melt the dark cooking chocolate with the butter in a saucepan over a low heat. When it is fully melted, but not too piping hot, drizzle it all over the brownie, then carefully spread it out using the back of a spoon to create a very thin layer of chocolate all over the surface. Put it back in the fridge. The layer is so thin that you might see the white slightly come through in patches – don't worry about it.

When this top layer of chocolate is solid, cut the brownie into 3cm squares with a sharp knife.

Because of the butter in the top two layers, these need to stay in the fridge until just before serving.

When our daughter arrived early our beloved friend, Emily, got on a plane from New York to make us food and look after us. She is such a soulful cook and always seems to know about the good shit in life first. She sends us care packages from the States, with spices for me and jumpers she has knitted for our kids, along with our now-favourite books. We all love to read *Thunder Cake* by Patricia Polacco – a story about a young girl who overcomes her fear of Michigan thunderstorms when her grandmother takes her outside on their farm to collect ingredients for a cake as a storm approaches. For me, it is about the power of preparing food. This is Emily's family dessert.

thunder cake (swedish oven pancake)

SERVES 6

120g plain flour, sifted
½ tsp salt
1 tbsp caster sugar
4 eggs
500ml whole milk
2 tbsp unsalted butter
pancake toppings of choice
  (such as yoghurt, stewed
  fruit, jam, maple syrup, fried
  bacon)

Preheat the oven to 200°C fan.

Combine the dry ingredients with the liquid in a large jug or bowl and whisk until completely blended.

Melt the butter in a cast-iron skillet or 23cm ovenproof frying pan over a medium heat. Pour in the batter, transfer to the oven and bake for 30 minutes, until puffy and golden brown on top.

Remove from the oven and slice the pancake into portions. Serve immediately with stewed fruit, or jam, maple syrup and yoghurt.

My wife introduced me to her mother on our third or fourth date and, coming from my chaotic family background, I nearly had a total meltdown beforehand. There was nothing to worry about – Diane is the coolest lady I know, and has completely and utterly had my back from the second I met her. It's hard to describe how much I like being around Diane, so I will just say that I love being cooked for by her. She rarely measures anything or follows a recipe, but feels her way with food and can throw things together for a crowd – a common thing in her house – without breaking a sweat.

This is one of my all-time favourite desserts. Diane grows rhubarb on her allotment, and we have an absolute abundance of it in the spring. This crumble gets made a lot at home and it rarely even makes it out of the dish and into a bowl: my wife and I stand over the kitchen island and eat it steaming hot. When we are being civilised and serve it 'mindfully', it is perfect with vanilla ice cream and a splash of olive oil.

There are some different opinions in the family about the fruit-to-crumble topping ratio – Diane likes more fruit, and Francesca is a topping fiend. I am happy either way. This recipe channels more Diane vibes, but you can increase your crumble ingredients to taste.

diane's rhubarb crumble

SERVES **6–8**

800g rhubarb, washed,
  trimmed and cut into 2.5cm
  lengths
100g caster sugar
ground cinnamon, for dusting
150g unsalted butter, plus
  extra for greasing
100g soft light brown sugar
160g rolled oats
60g ground almonds or plain
  flour

Preheat the oven to 180°C fan.

Lightly grease a casserole dish then add the rhubarb – you want enough to fill your dish about halfway. Sprinkle the caster sugar over the rhubarb and add a generous dusting of cinnamon.

To make the topping, melt the butter, then stir in the brown sugar, oats and ground almonds or flour. Sprinkle the topping over the rhubarb.

Bake the crumble for 30–40 minutes, until the rhubarb is bubbling at the edges and the topping is crunchy and golden brown.

Remove from the oven and serve.

Joan is my wife's aunt and a favourite person of everyone in our house. When Joanie comes to stay in London from California, we are all happy. These are her chewy molasses cookies. They stay soft for days (if they stick around that long) and the sparkling sugar tops and combination of spices make me think of American Christmas.

joan's molasses cookies

MAKES 24 COOKIES

165g unsalted butter
80g black treacle
1 tsp vanilla extract
1 egg
240g plain flour
150g caster sugar
2 tsp bicarbonate of soda
2 tsp ground ginger
2 tsp ground cinnamon
¼ tsp freshly grated nutmeg
¼ tsp ground cloves
¼ tsp fine salt
granulated sugar, for rolling

Melt the butter in a saucepan, then stir in the treacle and vanilla. Leave to cool before adding the egg to the mixture and gently stirring it through.

Mix the dry ingredients together in a separate bowl, then fold them into the butter mixture until you have a dough. Cover the bowl with cling film and refrigerate for at least 1 hour, to make the dough easier to shape. If the dough is chilled for longer than 2 hours, let it sit at room temperature for 30 minutes before rolling.

Preheat the oven to 180°C fan.

Roll the cookie dough into walnut-sized balls (about 1 tablespoon of dough per cookie), generously roll each ball in granulated sugar, then place on ungreased baking sheets 4–5cm apart, to allow for spreading.

Bake the cookies for 10 minutes or so, until the edges appear set. The cookies will puff up as they bake and then sink back down. If the tops aren't cracked, remove the baking sheet from the oven and gently bang it on the counter a couple of times, then return to the oven for one more minute. They should be soft so don't overcook them!

Remove from the oven and leave to cool on the sheets for 10 minutes before moving to a wire rack to cool completely. The cookies will stay good covered at room temperature for one week.

index

cookery conversions

weight

Imperial	Metric
¼ oz	10g
½ oz	15g
¾ oz	20g
1 oz	25g
1½ oz	40g
2 oz	50g
3 oz	75g
3½ oz	100g
4 oz	115g
4½ oz	125g
5 oz	150g
6 oz	175g
7 oz	200g
8 oz	225g
9 oz	250g
9½ oz	275g
10/11 oz	300g
12 oz	350g
13 oz	375g
14 oz	400g
15 oz	425g
16 oz (1 lb)	450g
1 lb 2 oz	500g (0.5kg)
1¼ lb	550g
1 lb 5 oz	600g
1½ lb	675g
1 lb 10 oz	725g
1¾ lb	800g
1 lb 14 oz	850g
2 lb	900g
2¼ lb	1kg

volume

Imperial	Metric	Imperial	Metric
1 fl oz (2 tbsp)	30ml	12 fl oz	350ml
2 fl oz	50ml	13 fl oz	375ml
3 fl oz	75ml	14 fl oz	400ml
3½ fl oz	100ml	15 fl oz (¾ pint)	450ml
4 fl oz	125ml	16 fl oz	475ml
5 fl oz (¼ pint)	150ml	18 fl oz	500ml
6 fl oz	175ml	20 fl oz (1 pint)	600ml
7 fl oz	200ml	1¼ pints (25 fl oz)	700ml
8 fl oz	250ml	1½ pints (30 fl oz)	850ml
9 fl oz	275ml	1¾ pints (35 fl oz)	1 litre
10 fl oz (½ pint)	300ml		
11 fl oz	325ml		

american cup conversions

American	Imperial	Metric
1 cup flour	5oz	150g
1 cup caster/ granulated sugar	8oz	225g
1 cup brown sugar	6oz	175g
1 cup butter/margarine/lard	8oz	225g
1 cup sultanas/raisins	7oz	200g
1 cup currants	5oz	150g
1 cup ground almonds	4oz	110g
1 cup golden syrup	12oz	350g
1 cup uncooked rice	7oz	200g
1 cup grated cheese	4oz	110g
1 stick butter	4oz	110g

spoons (liquids)

1 tsp	5ml	
1 tbsp	(3 tsp)	15ml

liquid conversions

½ fl oz	15 ml	1 tbsp
1 fl oz	30 ml	1/8 cup
2 fl oz	60 ml	¼ cup
4 fl oz	120 ml	½ cup
8 fl oz	240 ml	1 cup
16 fl oz	480 ml	1 pint

acknowledgements

There are a lot of people who worked on this book with me, and I want to sincerely thank them all. Before I do that, I'll start by saying something brief (but sad) about the family I was born into in California. My mother passed away a few years ago from illnesses related to alcohol and my youngest sister, earth-shatteringly, died a year later from an overdose. My other beloved little sister, who always supported me when she could, has her own struggles and I am currently unable to contact her. My father is in LA, and we try our very best with each other, sometimes fail but always try again. Starting with this information is just to say why I am so extremely grateful to the people around me, who anchor me in the world and have helped me create a life and meaningful work in England. I love to eat, and I love to cook, and writing a cookbook is something I have wanted to do for a long time. It feels unbelievably momentous to be here and it wouldn't have been possible without the support of the people below.

Firstly, thank you to my wife, **Francesca Zampi** – you are my family. You worked on this book as if it was your own, and kept the wolves from the door so we could create ADIP. To quote *The Fires of Heaven* by Robert Jordan: 'The oak fought the wind and was broken, the willow bent when it must and survived.' You are the willow, and your ability to adapt and stay calm and collected when I am generally not, and handle so many things at once, made this book, and so many wonderful things in our life, possible. You're the best thing that's ever happened to me, and I fall more in love with you every day.

Thanks too to my children **Thomasina** and **Hamilton** for completing my life, for making me laugh so hard every day, for watching my recipe videos and telling me whether they are good or not, and for making me a better person. You both find joy in doing almost anything, and I just want to be more like you both.

Next, I want to thank **Alice Russell,** my literary agent and manager. It is funny to call her that, as she is so much more than that to me and my family. Alice is my wife's closest friend, my kids' 'other mother', my son's actual godmother and truly the best person you could trust with your dreams and ambitions. I've seen Alice work on many brilliant books over the years I've known her, so I knew what it meant to have her in my corner. Extremely lucky. Alice made me believe I could do a cookbook; told me I was a good writer (which made me cry) and constantly helped me shape and refine my thinking. I am grateful that Alice agreed to take me on, despite knowing how intense I can be, and shepherded this book into being.

Lizzy Gray – from the moment we met I knew I wanted Lizzy to be my editor. Finding out that she was taking on the book was a moment I won't forget. So many of the books that she has fostered have helped me become the cook I am today. I worry about almost everything, but throughout this process I came back to the same mantra. 'it will be all right; I'll work it out with Lizzy.'

Julian Roberts – for giving his wealth of knowledge, and supreme taste and ideas to the design of this book. You don't get many excited-like-Christmas-morning feelings as an adult, but that's how it felt every time I got a PDF from Julian. He really looked after this book, and I can't thank him enough.

Florence Blair and **Emma Cantlay** – for food styling. Shooting on film meant that Florence couldn't see any of the images I was taking as we went, a challenge she took on with complete grace. Florence was able to make every plate she touched skilfully levelled up and watching her and Emma calmly cook 50 dishes in five days (making them look better than I ever could) was awe-inspiring.

Laura Nickoll – my copy editor – is a true legend with a deep well of patience. When Laura told me she has a teenage son I knew we would be totally fine together. The process of fine-tuning writing can be brain-breaking for me, but Laura knows food and always understood what I was trying to say, so we got through it together with snack breaks.

Thank you to **Anna Greenland** for having me (and my children!) at your house for a weekend and providing the beautiful vegetables we shot for the chapter headings and the cover. All these vegetables were grown by Anna and she helped me shoot them. We worked under completely chaotic circumstances with our kids around our ankles shouting at us, grabbing things and eating them as we were trying to shoot and generally being feral. I talk about Anna in the intro for her dessert but can say it again - she is the best person and I feel so lucky to be friends with her.

The team at Found – Molly Costello, Alice King, Maya Luthra, Lizzie O'Connell, Daisy Janes, Natoya Martin, Gee Burns, KJ Sullivan, Holly Hirsch: they are all legends, and I want to thank them for working so hard and always having my back.

FC – who brought me to London 17 years ago and gave me my first camera. These things changed the course of my existence, I don't think I would be alive if we hadn't met.

Diane Borger – my mother-in-law, who has talked to me about this book so much. Diane is a theatre producer and her life's work is to help people create – she has been there for me for all my creating, encouraging me, loaning me great cookbooks to read, listening to my worries, and talking to me about photography and style and what matters to me most.

Babe Borger – the bedrock of a long line of incredible women. When you're a child you see the grownups around you as all-knowing, and capable of anything. That's how I still see Babe. She's been here for damn near a century, and despite having faced some of the hardest realities that life can bring, she remains positive and unfailingly good-humoured. There are not many other places I would rather be, than at Dairy Queen in New Smyrna Beach gassing about food and life with Babe.

The Standing family – Sarah, Johnny, Archie, India and Tilly – who offered up your home to me when I first moved to London, adopted me as a stray and showed me what family can be. Sarah treated me like one of her own, made meals for me, taught me a thousand things about cooking, got me my first professional photo assignment, and then ultimately when I was 25 gave me the tough love I needed by telling me I wasn't welcome in her home again until I got sober, which I then did. I am so thankful.

Andrew Baptiste – for being my brother, taking my calls all day every day and talking me off the ledge when I have meltdowns. My life would be so much worse if he wasn't in it. Come hell or high-water Andrew is straight chilling ready to go, and I am so grateful to have him in my life.

Frederick Paxton – if I'm not on the phone with Andrew, it's probably Freddie I'm gabbing to. He's loaned insights from his immense talent as a photographer and director to everything I've worked on since I've known him. All while helping me be a better friend, husband and father. I would be lost without him.

Lowell Delaney and **Robie Uniacke** – they became my best friends in London and grew my love of food and cooking. They took me places like St. JOHN and Silk Road, and then Lowell showed me how to cook it all. She is the best cook I know, and I often think about whether she would like a recipe I'm working on. I fell in love with London because of them, and I'm not sure I would have stayed otherwise.

Jackson Boxer, for giving me a job in the kitchen at Orasay, **Gareth Saywell**, the head chef when I started, and **Vagelis Dagdelenis** who took over – they made me a better cook, taught me how to do things properly, called me chef, and changed the direction of ADIP for the better.

Richard Sharp – he knows why. Love chat makes Sharp uncomfortable, but he is such a good man, and we all love him so much. There would be no ADIP without him.

The people who helped me get my ADIP Instagram account going – my first few followers found me because of my friend **Shona Vertue** (thanks for that, mate). **Ed Smith** and **Ben Lippett** both did collabs with me when I had a very small account which is kindness that I won't forget.

Jamie Oliver – who has advised me, generously shared my Instagram account with his followers and encouraged me. From one dyslexic to another, I want to say thanks, bro. He helped me believe I could do this.

Alex Doherty – for loving my kids, being our extended family and always being a steadfast example of what a dad and man can be.

Richard Reed and **Nadia Troxler** – for being such good friends to me and Francesca and for letting me 'borrow' Richard's car for the last few years. I will probably give it back someday.

Rapid Eye – for always looking after my film and helping me print the pictures in this book.

Ray Burmiston – for making me his photography assistant when I didn't have a clue what I was doing, teaching me how to shoot on film, not firing me, and giving me a place to stay when the only other option was packing up and moving home. Early morning drives through London, listening to Thin Lizzy, eating bacon sandwiches, and watching him dance around set brought me great joy. I love you, Ray.

Charlotte (Tiggy) Burkeman – for getting me my first set of real knives, getting me to the hospital when I was very sick, visiting me there often, taking me to a fancy lunch the day before my surgery, and to the sea and then the mountains while I was healing.

Madeline Østile – for taking a chance on me and getting me my first fashion story.

Katie Grand – getting to work with Katie completely changed my career and put a spotlight on my directing and photography. Katie opened the door and put me in the middle of the room, and I'll never forget it.

Jeremy and **Annabelle Scholar** – for introducing me to Francesca.

People I love who I just want to say a general thank you to for their emotional support, talking to me about the book and some for giving me dessert recipes (people listed in alphabetical order): **Emily Alexander, Joan Borger, Paul Coulon, Adam and Daniel Desure, Cora and Felix Doherty, Yanuel Garcia, Elissa Goldstone, Jesse Gouveia, George Gyftakis, my sister Taaj Jenkins, my dad Steve Jenkins, Janina Joffe, Cathy Kasterine, Sadie Kirshman, Roland Keane, Gloria Lema, Lucy McIntyre, Gillie Moroney, Shane Murphy, Ronnie Mushiso, Matthew Nichols, Kurtis O'Connor, Cassandra Stavrou, Angela and Matt Stone, Olivia, George, Freya and Elodie Tapsfield, Charlie Tarr, Ottilie Windsor, Brian Woo, Alessandro Zampi** and **Giuliano Zampi.**

And finally, I want to acknowledge **my mother Cheryl** – even though she is no longer here. It was hard to have her as a mom, and it was even harder to go years without her throughout my childhood. She was the cook's favourite cook, and she shared her taste and crazy love for food with me. If I have any inherent touch for cooking, it's from her and I am grateful for it.

First published 2025 by Bluebird
an imprint of Pan Macmillan
The Smithson, 6 Briset Street, London EC1M 5NR
EU representative: Macmillan Publishers Ireland Ltd, 1st Floor,
The Liffey Trust Centre, 117–126 Sheriff Street Upper,
Dublin 1, D01 YC43

Associated companies throughout the world
www.panmacmillan.com

ISBN 978-1-0350-5333-9

7 9 8 6

A CIP catalogue record for this book is available from the
British Library.
Printed and bound in Germany

Design by Julian Roberts at Irving & Co
Typesetting by maru studio

Visit www.panmacmillan.com to read more about all our
books and to buy them. You will also find features, author
interviews and news of any author events, and you can sign
up for e-newsletters so that you're always first to hear about
our new releases.